LOVE and HEART

2

CHITOSE KAIDO

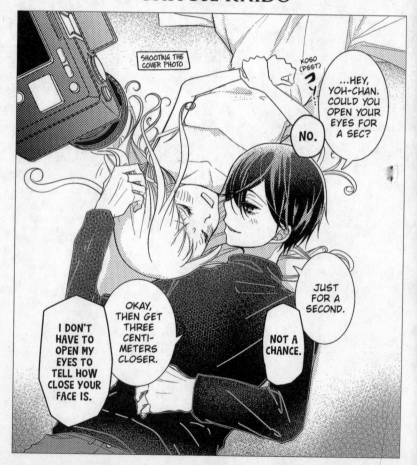

CONTENTS

LOVE AND HEART

14

ALL THIS TIME, YOU'VE BEEN THE ONLY THING I'VE EVER CARED ABOUT.

WHAT'S THE MATTER, AUNTIE...?

...YEAH, I'M ALL SET FOR MY STUDY ABROAD.

...WELL, I FINALLY GET TO GO BACK TO JAPAN.

GASA (RUSTLE)

...WHAT? I SOUND HAPPY?

I'LL MAKE SURE TO STOP BY THE HOUSE THE DAY THAT I LEAVE.

ANYWAY, I STILL HAVE PACKING TO DO.

YOU WORRY TOO MUCH.

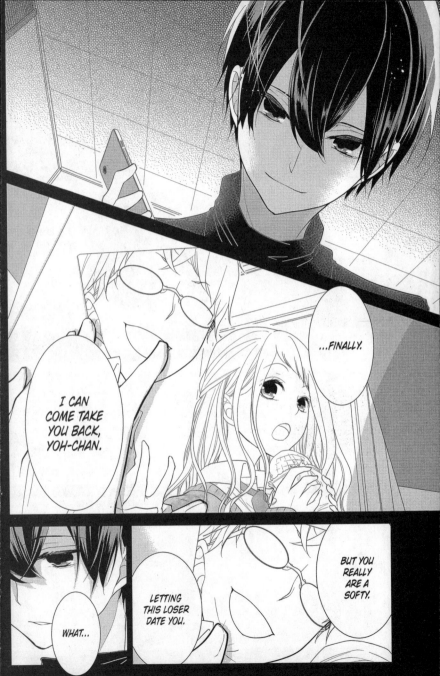

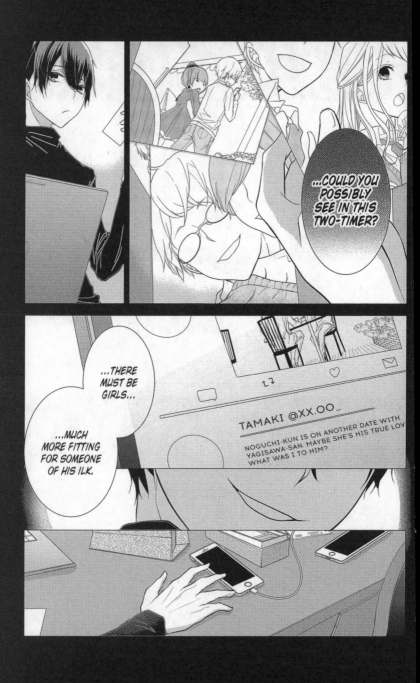

NICE TO MEET YOU.
MY CRUSH DOESN'T
LIKE ME BACK EITHER,
AND I COULDN'T HELP
FEELING LIKE WE'RE
KINDRED SPIRITS.
I WAS HOPING WE
COULD BE FRIENDS.

MY CRUSH DOESN'T
LIKE ME BACK EITHER,
AND I COULDN'T HELP
FEELING LIKE WE'RE
KINDRED SPIRITS.
I WAS HOPING WE
COULD BE FRIENDS.

THANK YOU.
I'D LOVE TO BE FRIENDS.

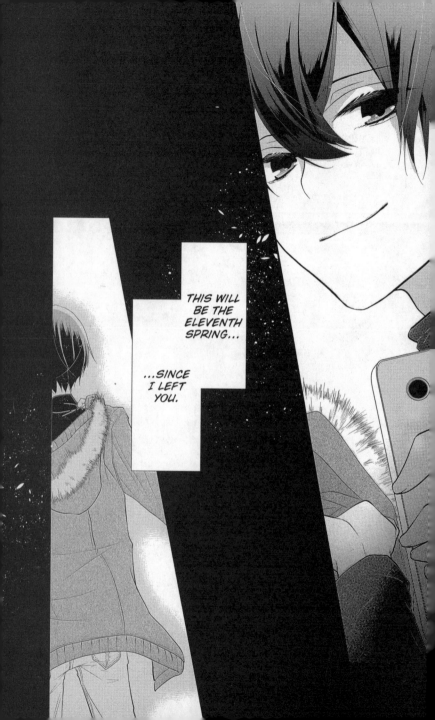

YOU CAME ALL THIS WAY, BUT MS. YAGISAWA IS IN A MEETING...

WILL ICED TEA BE OKAY?

I'M SORRY, HARUMA-KUN.

OH PLEASE, HARUMA-KUN! YOU'RE SO QUICK TO FLIRT...!

OH—

THAT'S FINE.

I WANTED TO TALK TO YOU TOO, SASAKI-SAN.

GASHAAAA (CRAAASH)

B...

I-I'M SO SORRY, HARUMA-KUN, ARE YOU ALL RIGHT !?

SU (SFF)

WORRY ABOUT YOURSELF FIRST, SASAKI-SAN.

YOU SHOULD GO GET CHANGED.

BUT ACTUALLY, I...

...WAIT, AAAACK!!

GURA (TIP)

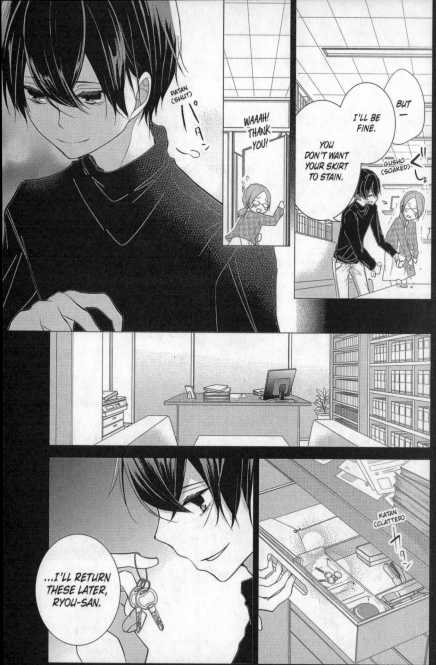

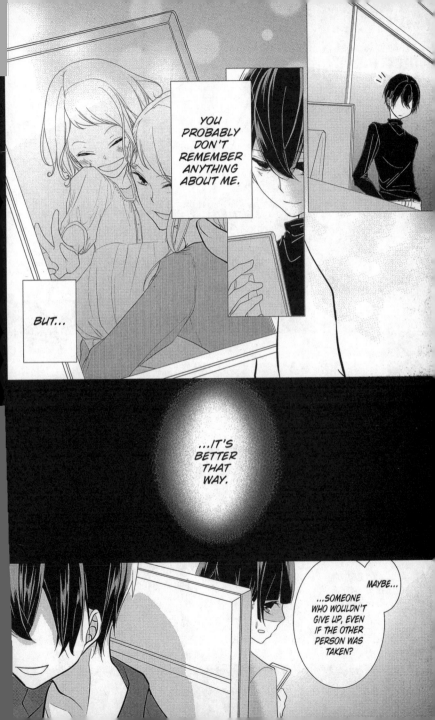

OH, SAWAKO. YOU NEED TO CATCH YOUR TRAIN.

WE'D BETTER GET GOING, THEN.

AWWW.

PIRON (DING)

GASP!

WHAT DO I DO? I TOLD NOGUCHI-KUN I DIDN'T SEND THE TEXT, BUT THE WAY THINGS ARE GOING, HE MIGHT FIND OUT IT WAS ME...

TOUYA, OUR CHECK!

ewe.

WHY NOT FOLLOW HER? IF YOU CATCH HER CHEATING, YOU CAN CONVINCE NOGUCHI-KUN YOU WERE RIGHT.

I DO FEEL BAD, YOH-CHAN...

...THAT I SCARED YOU BY GIVING YOU REASONS NOT TO TRUST ME.

BUT KNOWING HOW KIND AND RESPONSIBLE YOU ARE...

...IF YOU HAD SUSPICIONS ABOUT SOMEONE WHO TURNED OUT TO BE INNOCENT...

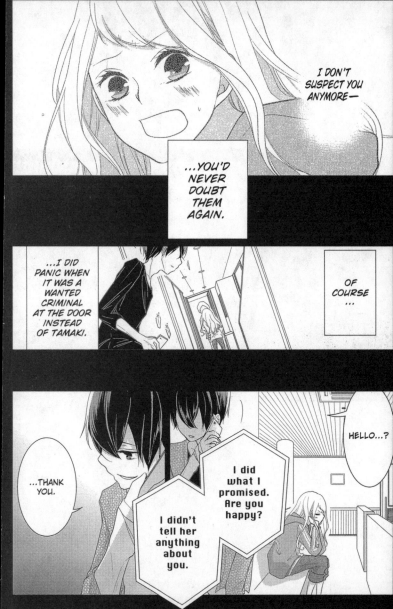

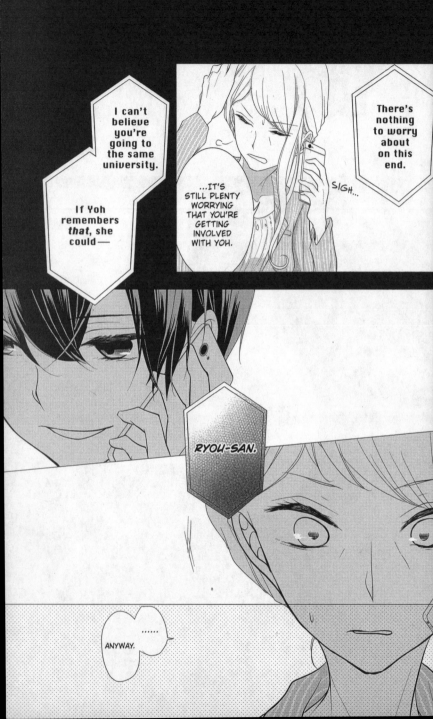

DON'T WORRY, RYOU-SAN.

HEH.

At least stop putting Yoh in harm's way.

I'LL KEEP YOH-CHAN SAFE.

EVEN IF YOU NEVER REMEMBER ME...

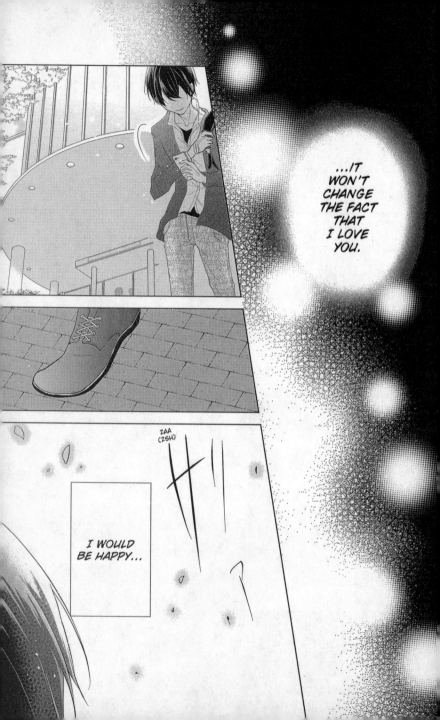

...IT WON'T CHANGE THE FACT I LOVE YOU.

ZAA
(ZSH)

I WOULD BE HAPPY...

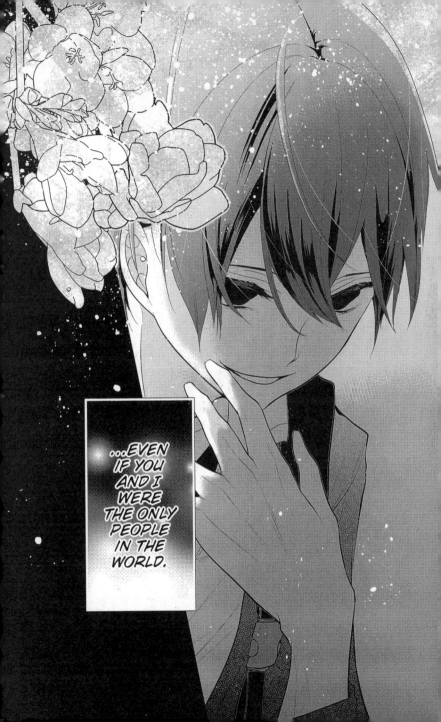

...EVEN IF YOU AND I WERE THE ONLY PEOPLE IN THE WORLD.

#15

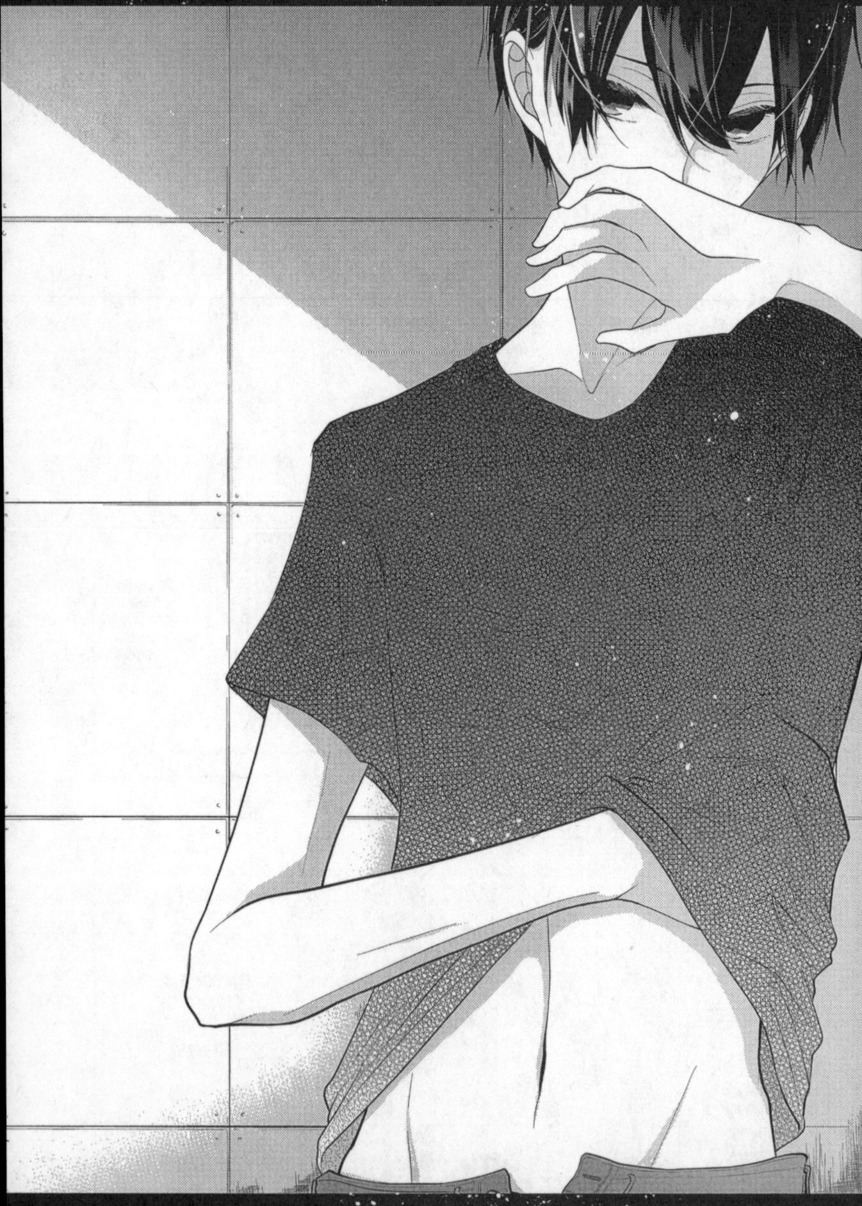

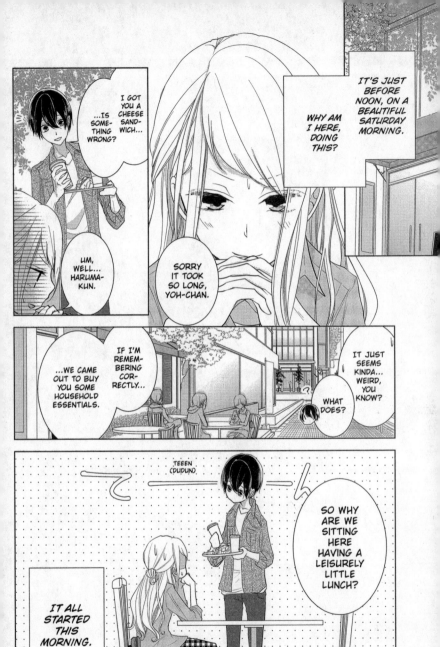

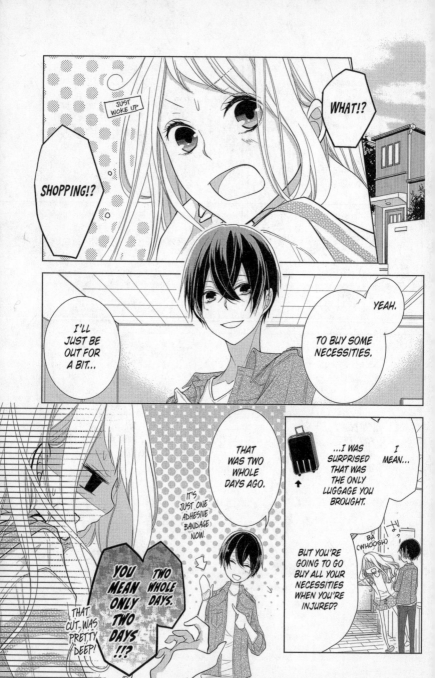

WHAT DO I DO...? HE MIGHT WANT TO SHOP BY HIMSELF, WITHOUT ANYBODY HOVERING.

BUT I'M WORRIED ABOUT HIS HAND...

HRRRM...

AND IT'S MY FAULT HE GOT HURT TO BEGIN WITH.

I DIDN'T BRING ANY BECAUSE I PLANNED TO BUY NEW ONES.

I DON'T HAVE ROOM ESSENTIALS OR A COMPUTER EITHER.

BUT I DIDN'T BRING THAT MANY CLOTHES, SO I HAVE TO GO SOON...

THIS SHOPPING TRIP IS EVEN BIGGER THAN I IMAGINED!!

HE'S SURE TO END UP LIKE THIS!!

BA (WHOOSH)

H-HARUMA-KUN!

I'LL GO W—

OH, I HAVE AN IDEA.

WHY DON'T YOU COME WITH ME, YOH-CHAN?

AND THAT'S WHAT HAPPENED, BUT...

I CAN WAIT FOR YOU TO GET READY.

...WHY ARE WE HAVING AN ELEGANT LUNCHEON?

I MEAN, YOU HADN'T HAD BREAKFAST YET, YOH-CHAN.

DON'T WORRY, I'M NOT IN A HURRY.

IT'S MORE BREAKFAST THAN LUNCH.

WELL, I'M GLAD, BUT...

ATTRACTING EVEN MORE ATTENTION BY SITTING OUTDOORS

ZAWA (MURMUR)

ZAWA

HARUMA-KUN! PLEASE UNDERSTAND HOW CONSPICUOUS YOUR FACE IS!

...SORRY. I MUST BE A BOTHER, AREN'T I?

DRAGGING YOU OUT SHOPPING ON SUCH SHORT NOTICE...

I WAS RUSHING WHEN I GOT DRESSED AND DID MY HAIR...

DOES THIS SITUATION NOT BOTHER HIM AT ALL...?

OH. IT'S NO TROUBLE...

21

I'LL DO MY BEST TO CARRY STUFF FOR YOU TODAY!

ACTUALLY, I'M SORRY FOR MAKING YOU TAKE CARE OF ME.

GATA (CLATTER)

MOGO (NOM)

HUH?

...I SEE.

SO DON'T WORRY ABOUT IT.

I'M USED TO IT. I GO SHOPPING WITH TOUYA A LOT.

IT NEVER FEELS LIKE THIS, THOUGH.

? ?

WHAT?

I WAS GOING TO HAVE ALL THE HEAVY THINGS SHIPPED.

BUT YOU SEEMED WORRIED, SO I THOUGHT YOU'D FEEL BETTER IF YOU COULD KEEP AN EYE ON ME.

WHA!? NO WAY!

AH HA HA.

I COULD NEVER ASK YOU TO DO THAT FOR ME, YOH-CHAN.

SO YOU DIDN'T ASK ME TO COME ALONG SO I COULD CARRY YOUR THINGS...?

22

BE-SIDES.

THIS IS FUN, RIGHT? IT'S LIKE A DATE.

YOU WOULD ACTUALLY SAY THAT NOW? ABOUT THIS?

WELL, SHALL WE GO?

YOU...

HEH.

23

COME TO THINK OF IT...

LET'S SEE. WE'LL BUY CLOTHES AND ESSENTIALS THERE, AND...

...I DON'T REALLY KNOW THAT MUCH ABOUT HARUMA-KUN...

HE DID TELL ME ABOUT HIS FAMILY, THOUGH...

I WOULDN'T BE SURPRISED AT ALL TO FIND OUT HE HAS A GIRLFRIEND...

HE REALLY IS USED TO THIS KIND OF THING...

MIND IF WE LOOK AT CLOTHES FIRST?

...SO.

WHAT WAS IT LIKE FOR YOU, LIVING OVERSEAS?

HUH?

YOU DO HAVE A POINT.

I DIDN'T REALLY MEAN ANYTHING BY IT.

UHH...

OH, UM.

IT'S JUST, I DON'T REMEMBER ANYTHING FROM OUR PAST, AND IT KIND OF MAKES ME FEEL LIKE I'M AT A DISADVANTAGE OR SOMETHING.

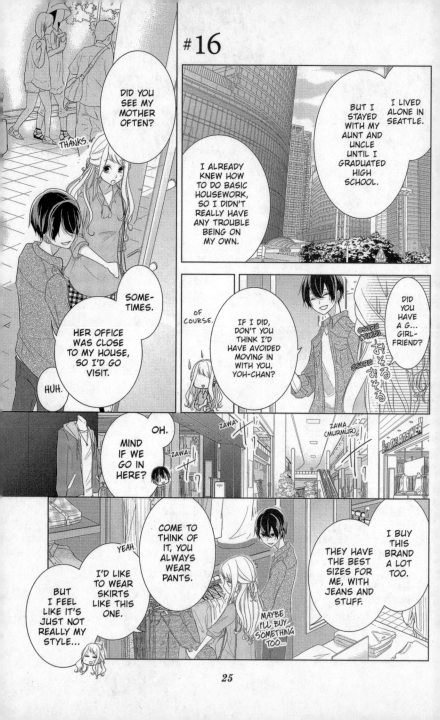

URK.

WHY NOT?

YOU'RE CUTE.

HEH.

WHAT'S WRONG WITH A GIRL WEARING PANTS!?

OH!

...YOU KNOW, HARUMA-KUN, THAT KIND OF TALK—

OH, WE'RE NOT—

WE HAVE LOTS OF OUTFITS...

YOU WANT A LOOK THAT MATCHES YOUR BOYFRIEND'S WITHOUT BEING TOO OBVIOUS, RIGHT!?

...FOR BOY-GIRL PAIRS!

IF THAT'S STILL TOO EMBARRASS-ING FOR YOUR BOYFRIEND, WHY NOT MATCH YOUR INNERWEAR?

LIKE A T-SHIRT AND CAMI-SOLE WITH MATCHING PATTERNS.

I SAID WE'RE NOT...!

PEOPLE REALLY NOTICE IT WHEN YOU'RE WEARING MATCHING TOPS.

BUT IT'S HARDER TO SPOT IF YOU MATCH THE JEANS INSTEAD.

SEXY POSE FOR NO REASON

TAKE IT OFF!?

EEEK! ♥

DON'T YOU JUST LOVE IT!?

THE ONLY ONE WHO'LL EVER KNOW YOU'RE WEARING MATCHING INNERWEAR... IS THE ONE YOU LET TAKE IT OFF...... ♥

GUI (YANK)

LISTEN FOR A SECOND!!

RIGHT? RIGHT?

I—

I'M TELLING YOU, IT'S NOT WHAT YOU THINK!

WE'RE NOT ACTUALLY...

ZUSHI (TROMP)
ZUSHI

HUH?

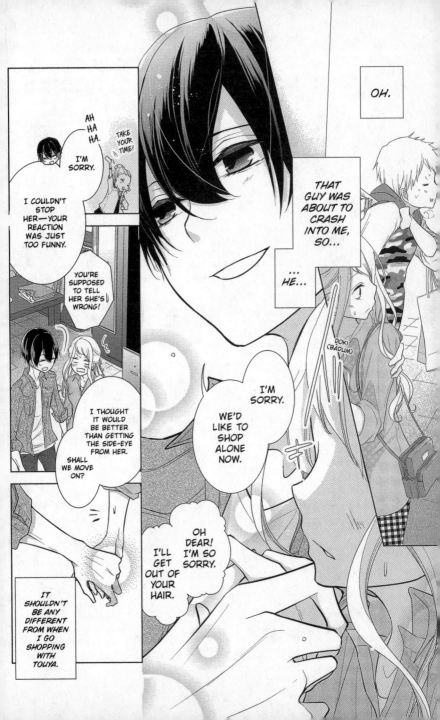

HE HOLDS MY HAND LIKE IT'S TOTALLY NATURAL.

BUT MY HEART IS BEATING FASTER THAN NORMAL, AND IT WON'T SLOW DOWN.

DOKI

ANYWAY, I'VE LEARNED...

...THAT HARUMA-KUN DEFINITELY HAS EXPERIENCE WITH THIS KIND OF THING.

DOKI

I WAS SO FOCUSED ON SHOPPING THAT I DIDN'T NOTICE...

WE DID A LOT OF GOOFING OFF!

BUT IT WAS A BIG HELP TO HAVE YOU HERE TO SHOW ME AROUND, YOH-CHAN.

ALMOST EVERY STORE I REMEMBERED IS GONE.

WHAT? NO WAY. IT'S ALREADY GETTING DARK!?

SIGN: BUS / TAXI

I MEAN, I'M NOT SURPRISED. THE LAST TIME I WAS IN JAPAN WAS MORE THAN TEN YEARS AGO.

I DIDN'T SEE A SINGLE PLACE THAT BROUGHT BACK ANY MEMORIES.

THE STREETS ARE ALMOST ALL DIFFERENT TOO.

...OH.

AND AFTER ALL THAT, THERE'S NOT A SINGLE PERSON OR PLACE HE REMEMBERS...

'COS, YOU KNOW, IF YOU TELL ME STUFF, MAYBE I'LL REMEMBER...

DO YOU HAVE ANY STORIES ABOUT ME?

UH... HEY.

RIGHT.

HIS MOTHER SUDDENLY PASSED AWAY.

AND JUST LIKE THAT, HE HAD TO GO LIVE OVERSEAS.

IT MUST HAVE BEEN REALLY HARD.

YOU DON'T HAVE TO TRY SO HARD TO CHEER ME UP. I'M FINE.

BUT —

ALL I NEED...

...IS FOR YOU TO KNOW WHO I AM NOW.

BUT...

SHUN (GLOOM)

...WHEN YOU REMEMBER SOMEONE, AND THEY DON'T REMEMBER YOU...

...DOESN'T THAT...

...MAKE YOU FEEL LONELY?

IF THERE WAS AT LEAST A PLACE WHERE HE HAS FOND MEMORIES...

...OH!

PITA (HALT)

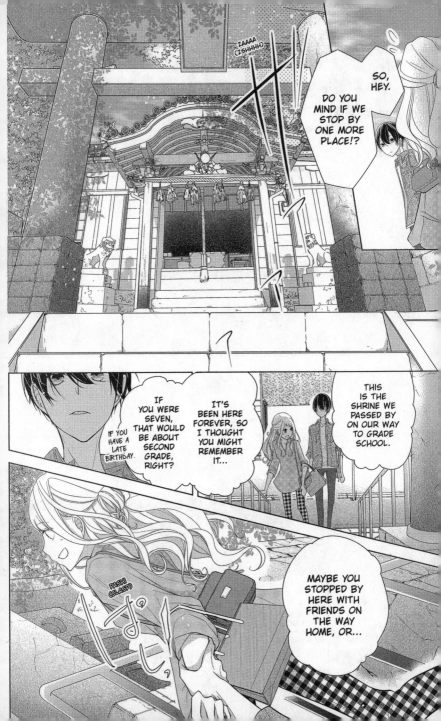

#17

...HARUMA-KUN...

...I DO REMEMBER THIS SHRINE.

I USED TO COME HERE ALL THE TIME.

...OH.

UH... OKAY. SORRY...

TAN (TMP)

TAN

YOU DIDN'T DO ANYTHING WRONG, YOH-CHAN.

BUT...

...IT'S NOT MY FAVORITE PLACE.

I BELIEVED IF I MADE A WISH HERE, IT WOULD COME TRUE...

...I USED TO COME HERE A LOT.

KATSUN (CLACK)

...I USED TO COME TO THIS SHRINE A LOT TOO.

...BUT NONE OF MY WISHES WERE EVER GRANTED.

SO ALL THE OLD ME EVER DID WAS BEG TO THE GODS.

I HAD NO ONE ELSE TO TURN TO.

I'D PRAY THAT SHE WOULDN'T STOP LOVING ME.

I'D PRAY THAT MOM WOULD COME HOME SOONER, EVEN BY JUST A FEW MINUTES.

...I WONDER...

UM...HEY, HARUMA-KUN.

IF HE WAS, THEN...

ZAAA CZSHHHD

...IF HARUMA-KUN WAS JUST LIKE ME.

ER...I MEAN...

I DON'T THINK I'LL BE MUCH HELP EXCEPT FOR HOUSEWORK AND SHOWING YOU AROUND TOWN.

AND IT'S NOT REALLY SOMETHING I SHOULD BE SAYING AFTER GETTING YOU HURT.

AWA (FLUSTER)

あ あ あ

HARUMA-KUN.

YOU CAN RELY ON ME TOO, OKAY?

BUT I WAS ALONE A LOT AS A KID TOO.

SO I GUESS, LIKE, I CAN KIND OF UNDERSTAND HOW YOU FEEL...

ZAAA

THE OTHER DAY, YOU TOLD ME I COULD TALK TO YOU ABOUT ANYTHING.

BUT NOW I HAVE TOUYA AND MY OTHER FRIENDS, SO WE CAN ALL...

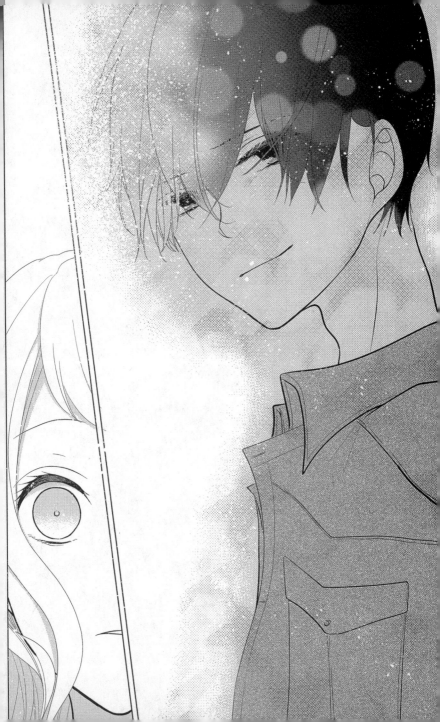

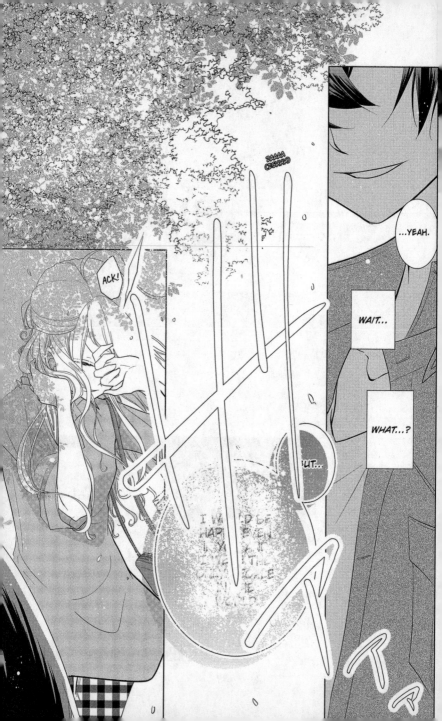

THAT WAS A BIG GUST...

......?

ZAAAA (ZSHHH)

I...I'M SORRY. WHAT DID YOU SAY...?

IT WAS NOTHING.

IT'S GETTING DARK. SHOULD WE GO HOME?

...NEVER MIND.

FOR A SECOND...

BA (WHOOSH)

PPPPPPP (RRRRRING)

HEY, HARUMA-KUN—

...HARUMA-KUN LOOKED LIKE HE WAS ABOUT TO CRY.

BUT WHY...?

IS IT REALLY BECAUSE I DON'T REMEMBER HIM?

SERIOUS (MOOD) DESTROYED

PIRIRIRIRD

PIRIRIRIRIRD

SORRY. MY PHONE...

...OH. IT'S TOUYA.

HEY, WHAT'S UP?

SHOPPING TOMORROW? NO THANKS. I'VE BEEN WALKING ALL DAY TODAY, AND I'M TIRED. NOW? I'M OUT OF THE HOUSE.

YOU SURE ARE CLOSE.

YOU AND TOUYA-SAN.

IS THAT ALL HE WANTED?

HUH?

I THINK IT'S NORMAL FOR FRIENDS...

OH, BUT...

THE DAY SHE MET SAWAKO

BUT YOU'RE TOO CLOSE FOR THAT!

YOU'RE NOT DATING!?

REALLY?

YEAH, SAWAKO SAID SOMETHING ABOUT THAT TO ME TOO.

...EVEN THOUGH HE'S ALWAYS JOKING ABOUT EVERYTHING, HE'S THE FIRST TO WORRY IF ANYTHING HAPPENS.

AND HE'S MORE CARING THAN ANYBODY NEEDS TO BE. I COUNT ON HIM FOR THAT.

OF COURSE, MOST OF THE TIME HE'S COMPLETELY USELESS.

HE'S ALWAYS DITCHING CLASS AND NEVER DOES HIS HOMEWORK.

HMPH.

...I SEE.

IF HE'S CARING PURELY BECAUSE YOU'RE FRIENDS, THEN OKAY.

PA (WHIRL)

HUH?

OH YEAH, YOH-CHAN.

I THINK THAT WOULD BE OKAY...

...BUT WHERE IS THIS COMING FROM?

WHY NOW?

OH.

IT'S JUST THAT SAWAKO-SAN GAVE ME HER NUMBER WHEN WE WENT TO THE IZAKAYA.

SO IT'S BUGGING ME THAT I STILL DON'T KNOW TOUYA'S...

*SEE CH. 3

THAT CONNIVING LITTLE...

WOULD YOU MIND GIVING ME TOUYA-SAN'S PHONE NUMBER?

I FORGOT TO ASK HIM THE OTHER DAY.

AND SINCE HE'S ONE OF MY NEW JAPANESE FRIENDS AND ALL...

...I FIGURED...

...IT'D BE NICE TO GET TO KNOW HIM BETTER.

New Student Roster

110042		
110043	HIROS	
110044	MANO,	
110045	MERA, AKIKO	
110046	YAGISAWA, YOH	
110047	YAMASHITA, AOI	
110048		
110049		

...WELL.

NIYA (SMIRK)

LOOK WHAT I FOUND. ♪

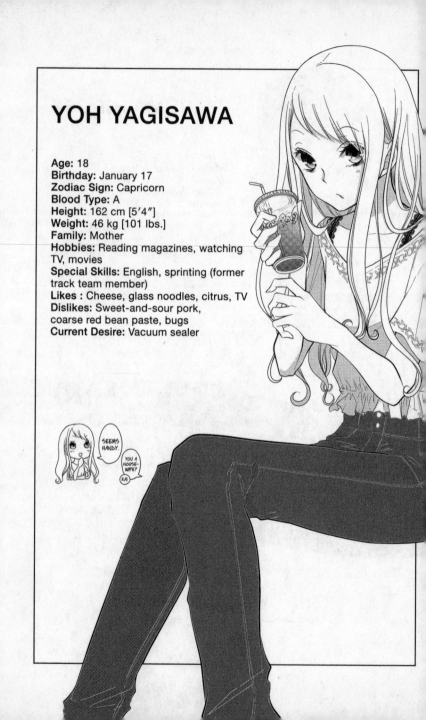

YOH YAGISAWA

Age: 18
Birthday: January 17
Zodiac Sign: Capricorn
Blood Type: A
Height: 162 cm [5'4"]
Weight: 46 kg [101 lbs.]
Family: Mother
Hobbies: Reading magazines, watching TV, movies
Special Skills: English, sprinting (former track team member)
Likes : Cheese, glass noodles, citrus, TV
Dislikes: Sweet-and-sour pork, coarse red bean paste, bugs
Current Desire: Vacuum sealer

SEEMS HANDY.

YOU A HOUSE-WIFE?

KAI

HARUMA HIROSE

Age: 18
Birthday: March 16
Zodiac Sign: Pisces
Blood Type: AB
Height: 179 cm [5′10″]
Weight: 63 kg [139 lbs.]
Family: Uncle, aunt, cousin
Hobbies: PCs, reading
Special Skills: Nothing in particular
Likes: Yoh-chan
Dislikes: Anything not Yoh-chan
Current Desire: Yoh-chan

YOU DIDN'T EVEN TRY FOR THE SECOND HALF. KAI

CAN I GO NOW?

...WAITING FOR ME.

YOH-CHAN IS...

#18

JUNE

IT'S BEEN SOME TIME SINCE THE WHIRLWIND OF CHAOS THAT WAS APRIL.

MY MOTHER WAS RIGHT.

IF I KNOW YOU, YOU CAN HANDLE IT.

I'M LIVING LIFE WITH EVERYTHING I COULD ASK FOR AND NOTHING TO COMPLAIN ABOUT.

BATA (STOMP)

BUT I'M THE ONLY ONE.

SORRY, I OVER-SLEPT!!

IT'S MY TURN TO MAKE BREAK-FAST...!

BATA

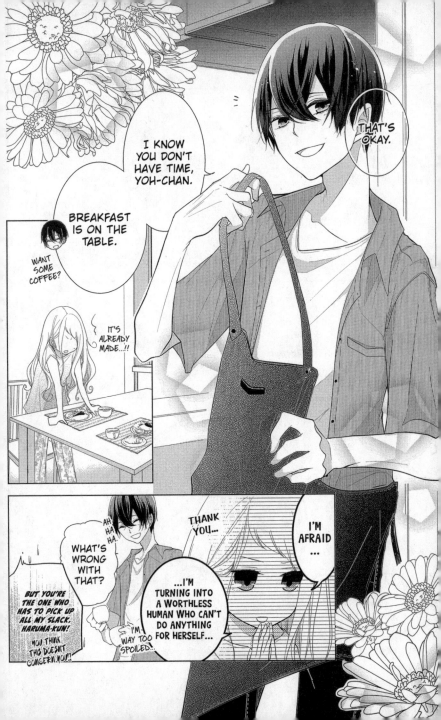

...THAT PART OF HIM SURE HASN'T CHANGED.

I PREFER TO BE THE ONE HELPING.

NO, THAT'S THE PROBLEM...

GASHA (KA-CHAK)

WAIT, HARUMA-KUN. I THOUGHT YOU DIDN'T HAVE CLASS UNTIL SECOND PERIOD...

I DON'T.

I WAS THINKING I'D HANG OUT IN THE LIBRARY UNTIL CLASS STARTED.

AND FOR YOU, YOH-CHAN, I'LL DO ANYTHING.

KOTO (CLUNK)

DO YOU NOT WANT ME TO WALK TO SCHOOL WITH YOU?

...BUT HARUMA-KUN HAS BEEN SPENDING A LOT MORE TIME WITH ME LATELY.

NO, IT'S FINE...

OH, GOOD.

THEN LET'S GO.

GACHA (KACHAK)

IT'S KIND OF NICE BUT EMBARRASSING.

AND THINGS ARE FEELING JUST A LITTLE WARMER THAN IN SPRING.

I'M TELLING YOU, IT'S DEFINITELY NOT WORTH TRYING.

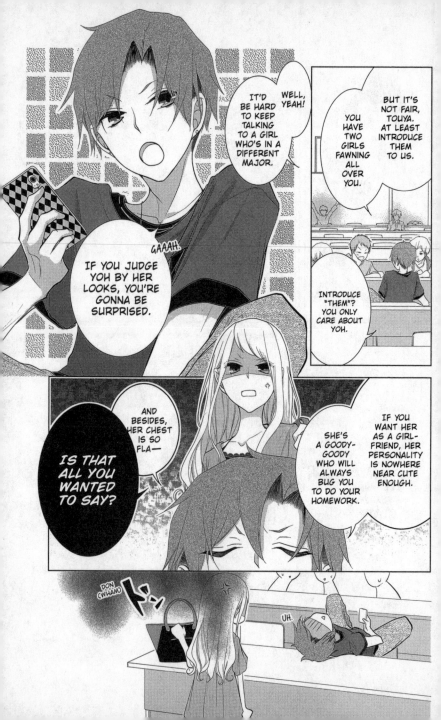

GOOD MORNING

?

OH, RIGHT, YOU'RE THEIR FRIEND TOO.

WE'RE TALKING ABOUT HOW THOSE TWO ARE SUCH CLOSE FRIENDS.

SOROO (SNEEEAK)

MORNIN'! WHAT'S UP?

WHO DO YOU HAVE TO THANK THAT YOU GRADUATED HIGH SCHOOL, HUH!?

IS THAT HOW YOU TALK ABOUT YOUR BEST FRIEND!?

NO, I'M TALKING ABOUT AS A GIRL-FRIEND.

THAT'S EVEN WORSE!!

GYAA GYAA GYAA GYAA GYAA GYAA

I WOULD BET MONEY THAT THEY'RE GOING TO BE DATING SOON.

DON'T WORRY! YOU CAN COUNT ON ME!!

I TOTALLY GET WHAT YOU'RE SAYING!

...YEAH.

BOSO (MUTTER)

CAN SHE EVEN TAKE A HINT...?

ARE YOU SURE...?

DON'T BE A THIRD WHEEL, SAWAKO. GIVE THEM SOME ALONE TIME SOMETIMES.

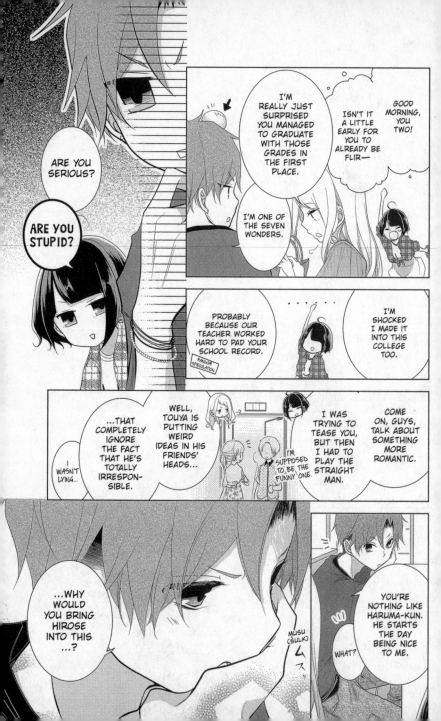

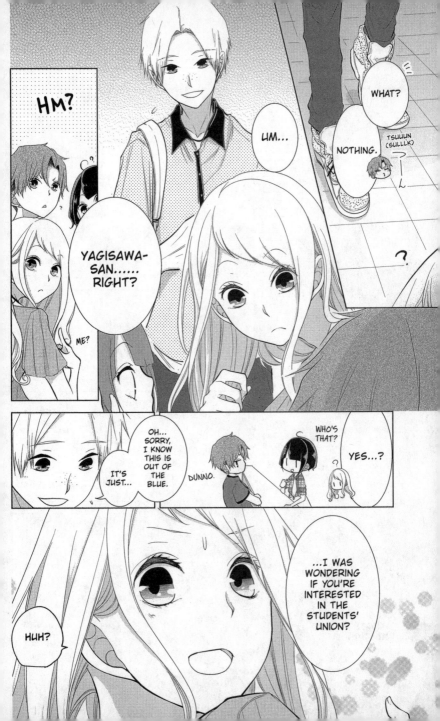

...HEY, SAWAKO, WHAT'S THE STUDENTS' UNION?

IT'S LIKE THE STUDENT COUNCIL, BUT FOR COLLEGE.

THEY PLAN ALL THE SCHOOL EVENTS, LIKE CULTURE FESTIVALS AND RECREATIONAL ACTIVITIES AND STUFF...

THAT'S RIGHT.

THE THING IS, I HAVE A SENPAI WHO SAID HE WANTED TO INVITE YOU, YAGISAWA-SAN.

MAYBE YOU KNOW HIM? A GUY NAMED KUNIE-SENPAI—

KUNIE-SENPAI!?

GATATA (CLATTER)

WHOA!

INTRODUCE ME TO HIM!!

NO WAY, YAGISAWA-SAN! YOU KNOW HIM?

SINCE WHEN!?

KUNIE-SENPAI? YOU MEAN THE SEXY VICE PRESIDENT OF THE STUDENTS' UNION!?

WHO...?

DO (SHOCK)

WAIT JUST A—

WAIT. WHO IS THIS PERSON? SOMEONE YOU KNOW, SAWAKO!?

NO, BUT EVERYONE IN THE SCHOOL KNOWS WHO HE IS!

I HEARD HE WAS VICE PRESIDENT LAST YEAR TOO, AND EVERYONE LOVED ALL OF HIS EVENTS.

HE'S GOT A LOT OF MODEL FRIENDS TOO, RIGHT?

ANY GIRL WHO COULD DATE HIM WOULD INSTANTLY BE A PRINCESS.

NOT ONLY IS HIS FAMILY LOADED, HE'S SUPER HOT AND A REALLY NICE GUY.

HE POSTS PICTURES ON SOCIAL MEDIA ALL THE TIME, AND HE KNOWS ALL THE TRENDS.

HIS CARS AND ACCESSORIES ARE ALL FROM HIGH-END BRANDS.

2711 LIKES.

YOU SAID THE SAME THING ABOUT HIROSE.

THE POINT IS, HE'S HOT!

I WISH!

...SO WHY WOULD A GUY LIKE THAT WANT ANYTHING TO DO WITH ME?

I DON'T RECALL EVER MEETING HIM.

?

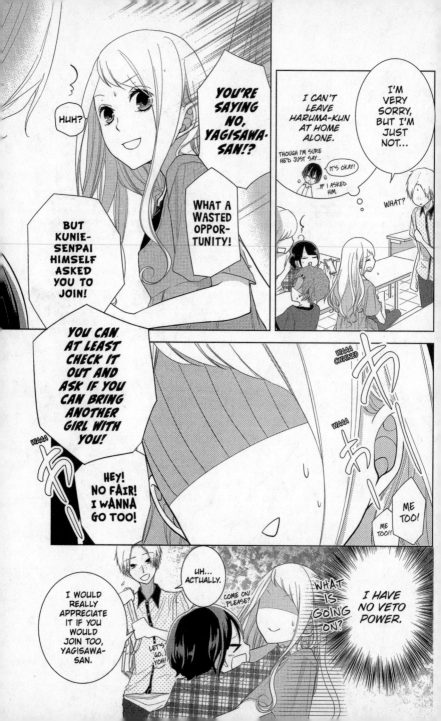

GASH! (CLAMP)

UH...WELL, IF IT'S JUST FOR A LITTLE WHILE...

COME ON, YOH! COME ON!

WE'RE SHORT-HANDED, AND THINGS ARE REALLY HECTIC RIGHT NOW...

EVEN IF YOU ONLY COME HELP TEMPO-RARILY...

THANK YOU! YOU'RE A LIFE-SAVER.

YOU'LL DO IT!?

UM...

PA (SPIN)

...HUH...?

OKAY, COME TO THE STUDENTS' UNION ROOM TOMORROW AT SIX O'CLOCK!

...MAYBE I IMAGINED IT.

...BUT IT FELT LIKE HIS HANDS WERE SHAKING...

HEY, YOH.

YOU DON'T MEAN THAT. YOU JUST GOT RAILROADED INTO IT.

I DON'T SEE WHY YOU CAN'T.

IT WILL BE ONE MORE PERSON TO HELP.

LUCKY.

DO YOU MIND IF I GO WITH YOU TOMORROW?

MUST BE ROUGH BEING SUCH A GOODY TWO-SHOES. YOU CAN'T SAY NO.

ARE YOU SURE ABOUT THIS? YOU WERE ABOUT TO SAY NO, WEREN'T YOU?

YAY!

YOU'RE LUCKY, SAWAKO!

IS THAT SUPPOSED TO BE PAYBACK?

HEH.

WHAT AM I SUPPOSED TO DO? THEY REALLY NEED THE HELP.

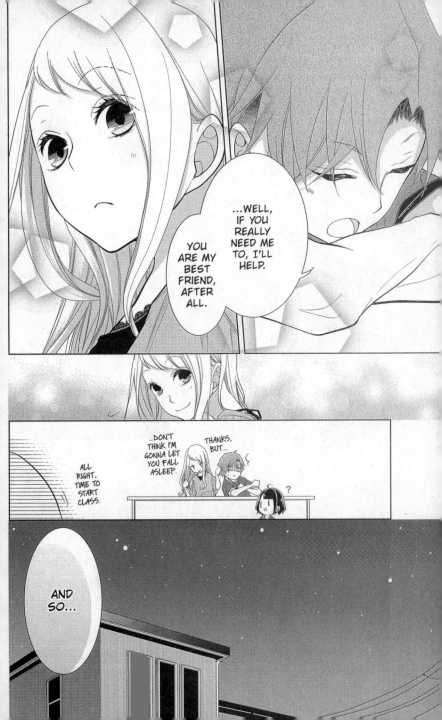

TOTAL VICTIM...

...OF CIRCUMSTANCE.

BUT I MIGHT BE COMING HOME LATE FOR A WHILE...

...I'M SORRY, HARUMA-KUN.

BUT THE STUDENTS' UNION, HUH...

HMMM.

EXACTLY WHAT I THOUGHT YOU'D SAY...

WHEW...

NIKO GGRIND

I SEE. THAT'S OKAY.

I WAS SUPPOSED TO MAKE BREAKFAST THIS MORNING. I'M MAKING UP FOR IT BY MAKING DINNER...

...AND WHY ARE YOU TRYING TO HELP ME WITH DINNER?

I WAS BORED, SO I FIGURED I'D HELP.

BUT I GUESS THAT WOULD BE TRICKY, WITH ME BEING AN EXCHANGE STUDENT.

I'D LIKE TO HELP TOO, IF I COULD.

NOW THAT I THINK OF IT...

I'LL GO AHEAD AND WIPE DOWN THE TABLE.

YOU'RE MAKING ME INTO AN UTTERLY WORTHLESS HUMAN BEING...

YOU THINK I WOULD STAND BY AND LET YOU HELP ME EVEN MORE...?

WHY DO YOU WANT TO KNOW?

I WAS INVITED, AND SAWAKO SAID SHE'S GOING TOO...

NO?

...WILL TOUYA-SAN BE GOING WITH YOU?

OH, JUST... YOU KNOW.

HEY, TOUYA-KUN.

WAI (CHATTER)

WAI

BIKU (JOLT)

ARE YOU DONE WITH YOUR BREAK YET?

GAYA (CLAMOR)

GAYA

SIGN: IZAKAYA MARUYA

21:40

HARUMA HIROSE

DO YOU HAVE SOME TIME TOMORROW NIGHT?

21:

WAI

YEAH... SORRY.

I'LL BE RIGHT THERE.

WAI

WHAT IS IT? A TEXT FROM YOUR GIRLFRIEND?

MUST BE NICE GOING TO COLLEGE, HAVING FUN EVERY DAY.

...FUN? I WOULDN'T SAY THAT...

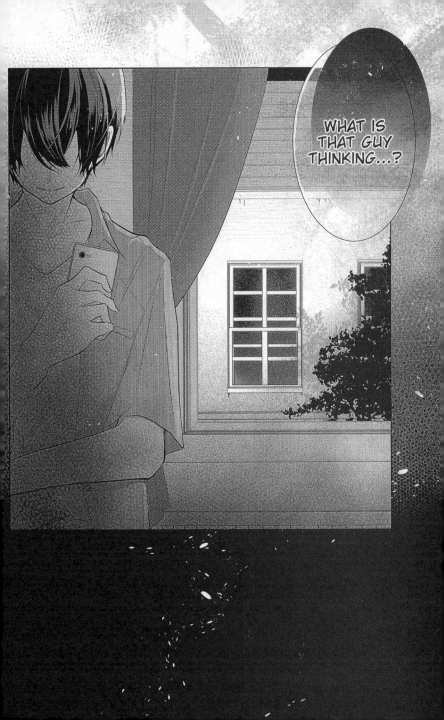

#20

THE NEXT DAY
STUDENTS' UNION
LET'S SEE...
I GUESS THIS IS THE STUDENTS' UNION ROOM.
ARE YOU SURE WE DON'T NEED TO COME WITH THE GUY WHO TALKED TO US YESTER-DAY...?
I LOOKED FOR HIM, BUT I COULDN'T FIND HIM!
KON KON (KNOCK)
OH, IT'S FINE. YOU WERE INVITED BY KUNIE-SENPAI HIMSELF.
I'VE ONLY SEEN HIM ONCE FROM AFAR SINCE SCHOOL STARTED. I CAN'T WAIT TO MEET HIM IN PERSON.
MAYBE I'LL ASK FOR HIS NUMBER.
THAT'S ALL YOU CARE ABOUT...
SAWAKO, HURRY AND OPEN THE D—
GACHA (KACHAK)
ARE YOU TALKING ABOUT ME?

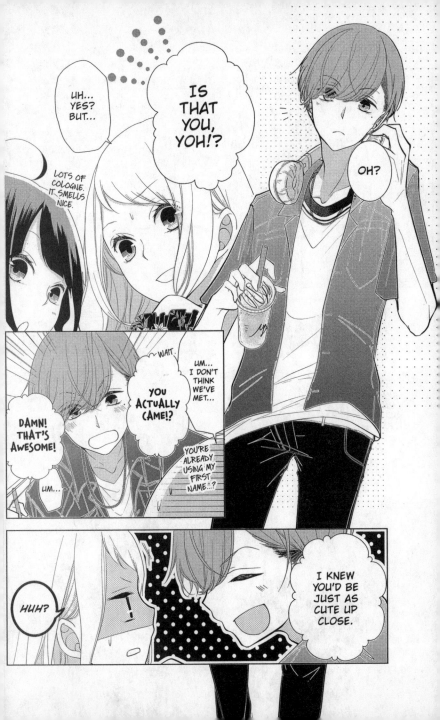

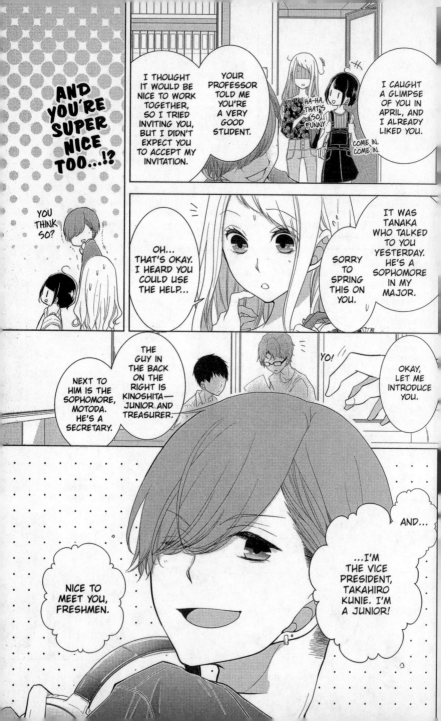

...MYSELF TOGETHER.

GOTTA PULL...

AH...NO. THERE AREN'T.

BESIDES THOSE TWO...

N-NOW THAT I'M THINKING ABOUT IT, ARE THERE ANY OTHER MEMBERS?

WHAT?

THAT'S IT? THAT'S WHY HE ASKED ME...?

OKAY, SAWAKO!

I'M SAWAKO! I'M HERE TO HELP!

...MY FACE...?

BECAUSE HE LIKES...

AND OUR PRESIDENT'S A SENIOR. HE HAS TO FIND A JOB AND WRITE HIS THESIS, SO HE CAN'T MAKE IT OFTEN. WE'RE UNDERSTAFFED.

BUT PEOPLE HAVE PART-TIME JOBS, AND WE CAN'T FORCE THEM TO COME IN.

NORMALLY SIX OFFICERS

PRESIDENT
|
VICE PRESIDENT
|
TREASURER (2)   SECRETARY (2)
|
COMMITTEE REPRESENTATIVES

...BUT IT'S PRETTY MUCH JUST US OFFICERS WHEN IT COMES TO DAY-TO-DAY OPERATIONS.

FOR EVENTS, WE FORM A LARGER ACTION COMMITTEE WITH REPRESENTATIVES FROM THE NEIGHBORHOOD ASSOCIATION AND VOLUNTEERS...

LET'S DO WHAT WE CAN TOGETHER!

OKAY?

YOU'RE REALLY SAVING OUR BUTTS BY BEING HERE, YOH.

PON (PAT)

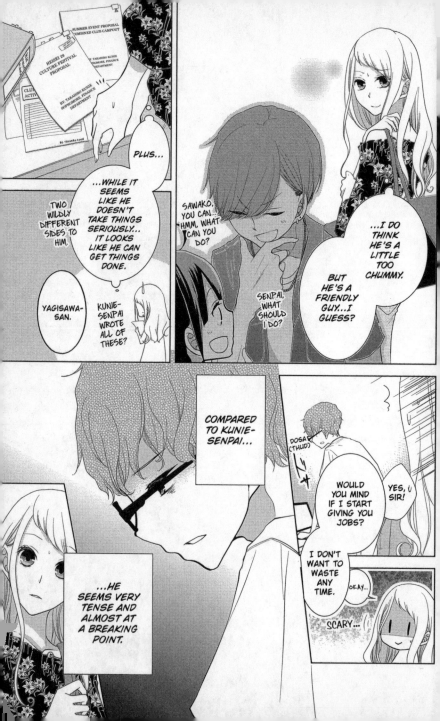

ACTU-
ALLY...

Y-YES!?

GIKU
(GULP)

CHIRA
(GLANCE)

I
DON'T
KNOW
WHY...

...BUT
THERE'S
A WEIRD,
HEAVY VIBE
HOVERING
AROUND
THESE
TWO...

...DID
KUNIE
ASK BOTH
OF YOU
TO JOIN
US?

WAI
(CHATTER)

HE
ASKED
ME.

SAWAKO'S
JUST
TAGGING
ALONG...

......

IF...

...HEY.

BOSO
(PSST)

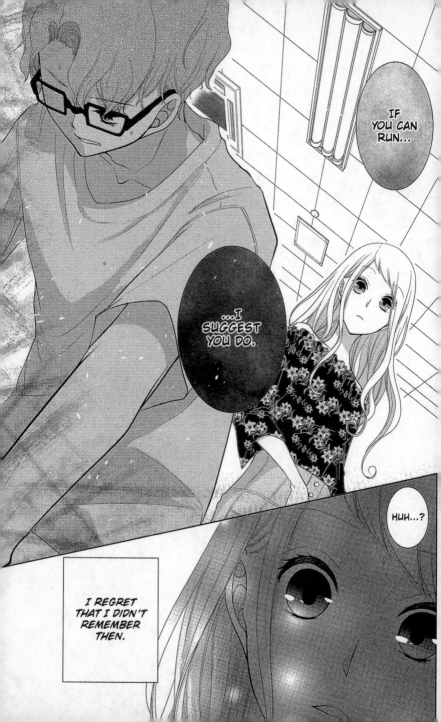

I GET SO BORED WHEN I DON'T HAVE WORK.

ALL MY OTHER FRIENDS ARE AT THEIR JOBS.

ARRRM.

YOH AND SAWAKO WENT OFF TO THE STUDENTS' UNION.

ABOUT HIM...

...OR HIS EVIL OBSESSION.

HI THERE.

OKAY, WHAT DO I DO NOW?

IF YOU'RE LOOKING FOR YOH, SHE'S AT THE STUDENTS' UNION...

UH... HI.

NO REASON, BUT...

URK!

NO.

TAJI (FIDGET)

GASP!

OH YEAH, THE TEXT YESTERDAY. I WASN'T SURE HOW TO RESPOND...

...SO I NEVER TEXTED BACK...!!

YOU'RE NOT DONE YET?

HMMM, HMMM.

AM I GHOSTING SOMEONE RIGHT NOW!?

HUH?

I WAS WAITING FOR YOU TODAY, TOUYA-SAN.

YOU NEVER ANSWERED MY TEXT YESTERDAY.

YOH-CHAN TOLD ME YOU DON'T HAVE WORK TODAY.

SO I CAME TO ASK YOU IN PERSON...

OH. SO HE'S NOT HERE TO YELL AT ME.

WHEW

SORRY TO SPRING THAT ON YOU.

UH... I... DIDN'T MEAN TO... SORRY,

WHEN I THOUGHT ABOUT IT, I REALIZED YOU HAD WORK YESTERDAY.

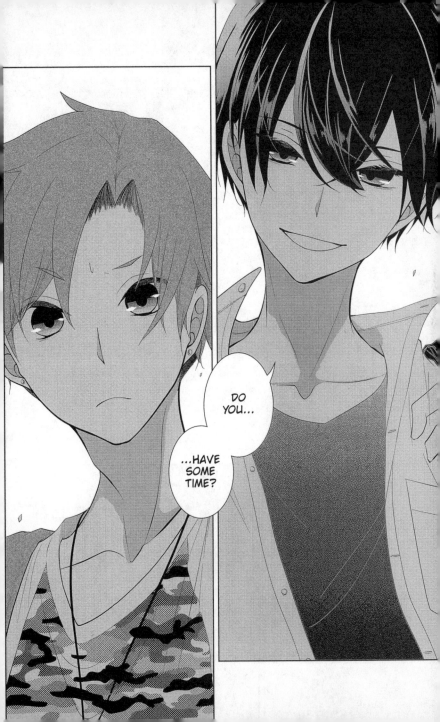

DO YOU...

...HAVE SOME TIME?

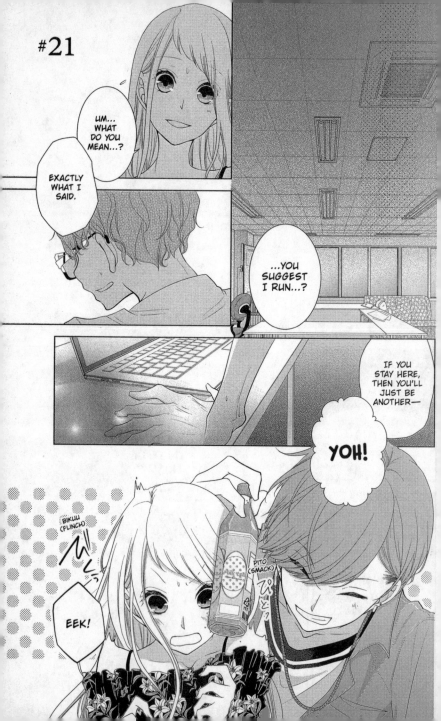

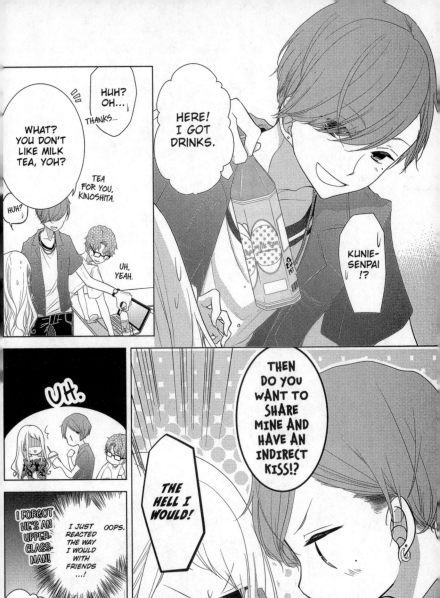

YOU'RE SO BASHFUL. IT'S ADORABLE. ♡

...HUH?

DOES THAT MEAN... HE WAS JUST JOKING AROUND ON PURPOSE?

SENPAI IS...

...SUPER GENEROUS!

OH...BUT SAWAKO...

KURU (WHIRL)

WANTED TO TALK TO YOU...

IF ALL WE NEED IS TO EXPLAIN HOW TO DO THE DATA ENTRY, YOU WANT ME TO DO IT?

...HE SEEMS SHALLOW, BUT HE MIGHT BE SURPRISING-LY MATURE...

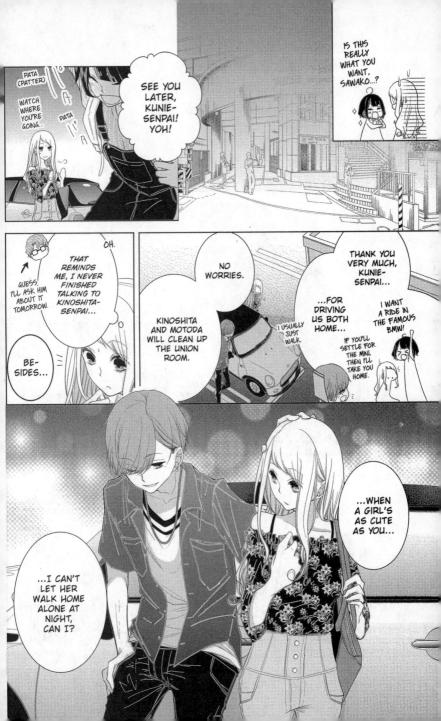

OH, COME ON, YOH.

UM, SENPAI. SERIOUSLY, YOU CAN STOP DOING THAT...

ARE YOU SAYING YOU CAN'T TRUST ME?

IF ONLY TOUYA WERE HERE NOW TO DEBATE HIM ON THIS SUBJECT...

...BUT A PRETTY FACE...

SHE'S NOTHING...

HAAH...

AND A GIRL WHO ISN'T AFRAID TO TALK BACK IS, LIKE, THE BEST.

YOU'RE PRETTY, AND THIN. YOU'RE EXACTLY MY TYPE.

YOU KNOW, I'VE ALWAYS HAD A THING FOR GIRLS WITH LONG HAIR.

OH...

I'VE RECENTLY DEVELOPED AN IMMUNITY TO GOOD LOOKS...

...REALLY? IS THAT YOUR ONLY REACTION?

EXCUSE ME?

WHEN A GUY AS HOT AS ME IS IN YOUR FACE, HITTING ON YOU?

FOR REAL!?

HARUMA-KUN IS THAT CLOSE TO ME ON A REGULAR BASIS.

WHAT DO YOU WANT TO EAT, YOH-CHAN?

TWO MONTHS' ACCUMULATION

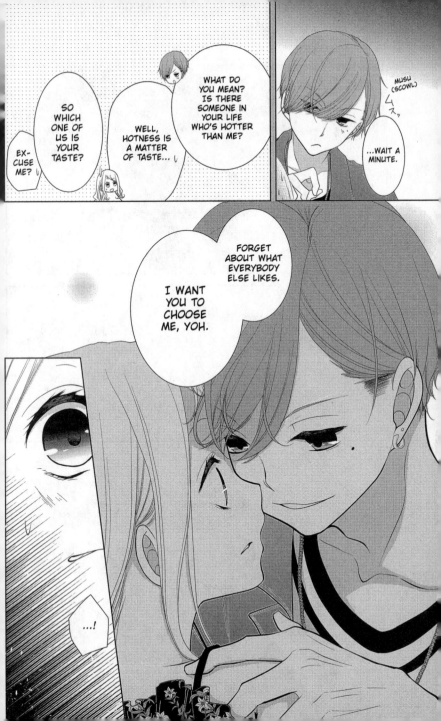

PESHI
(WHAP)

MEANT TO SHAKE HIS HAND OFF, BUT ACTUALLY HIT HIM

...UH.

NO WORRIES.

OH.

I-I'M SORRY. I DIDN'T MEAN TO HIT YOU.

I SLAPPED HIM!!?

THAT... THAT WAS DEFINITELY NOT GOOD!

WELL, I GUESS YOU'RE NOT THE KIND OF GIRL TO FALL FOR A GUY THAT EASILY.

SORRY ABOUT THAT. I GOT A LITTLE CARRIED AWAY.

I CAN SEE THAT PART OF YOU HASN'T CHANGED.

CHANGED...? I'M PRETTY SURE WE JUST MET TODAY AT—

THE WAY...

79

...YOU'RE SO DAMN FULL OF YOURSELF.

DO (WHAM)

!?

GA (GRAB)

I'M REALLY...

...SO RELIEVED TO SEE YOU HAVEN'T CHANGED.

YOH.

WHAT...? WHERE IS THIS ATTITUDE COMING FROM...?

BUT THAT WOULDN'T BE ENOUGH TO PAY YOU BACK...

I THOUGHT I COULD TAKE YOU TO, LIKE, A LOVE HOTEL...

...AND GET EMBARRASSING PICTURES OF YOU TO SHOW THE WORLD OR SOMETHING.

PIKU (TWITCH)

...P... PAY ME BACK...?

...DO YOU MEAN TO SAY YOU HONESTLY DON'T REMEMBER ME?

#22

IT WAS MY LAST YEAR OF HIGH SCHOOL.

AND YOU'RE THE ONE WHO STARTED IT.

HA HA HA HA HA!

SASA (CHURR?)

COME ON. NOBODY DOES THAT!

GYA HA HA HA HA!

SERIOUSLY!?

EXCUSE ME.

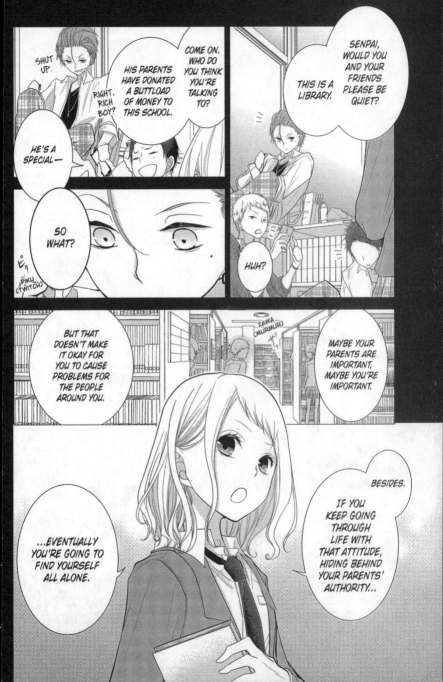

AAH!? WHAT'S HER PROBLEM?

...TO TRY AND CONFRONT ME IN PERSON.

YOU WERE THE ONLY IDIOT WHO WAS EVER COCKY ENOUGH...

IS THAT WHAT YOU WANTED?

THANK YOU.

I'M SORRY, YOH.

JUST SAYING SOMETHING WAS ENOUGH.

I WOULD NEVER, EVER FORGET...

...THE WOMAN WHO DAMAGED MY PRIDE.

ME TOO!

LUCKY! INTRODUCE ME!

KUNIE-SENPAI!?

I FOLLOWED YOUR ADVICE WHEN I GOT TO COLLEGE. ALL I HAD TO DO WAS PUT ON A FRIENDLY FACE...

WELL, I DO OWE YOU A LITTLE GRATITUDE.

...AND NOW THESE IDIOTS FLOCK TO ME FOR MY MONEY OR TO GET ON MY GOOD SIDE. I'M A SUPERSTAR.

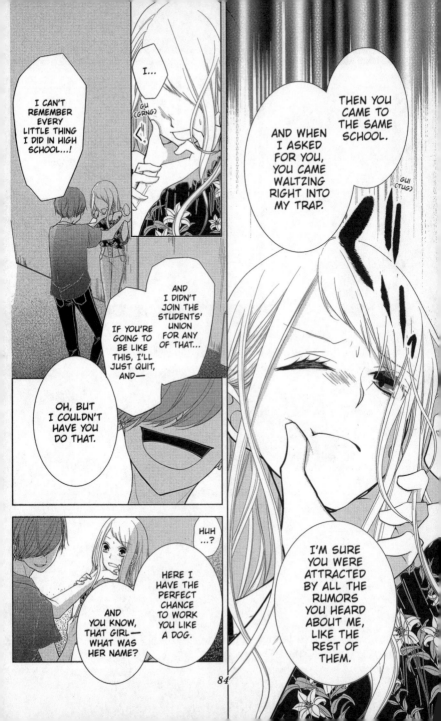

SAWAKO?

SAWAKO OKA
MESSAGE CALL LINE EMAIL

THE POOR THING. IF HER FRIEND QUITS THE UNION...

...SHE'LL HAVE TO PICK UP ALL THE SLACK.

WHETHER SHE WAS INVOLVED OR NOT...

...I DON'T CARE, AS LONG AS I CAN MAKE LIFE MISERABLE FOR YOU.

SAWAKO HAD NOTHING TO DO WITH—!

SO?

I MEAN...

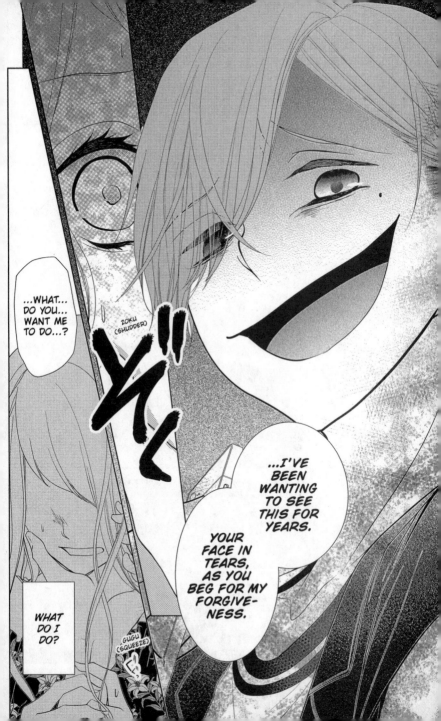

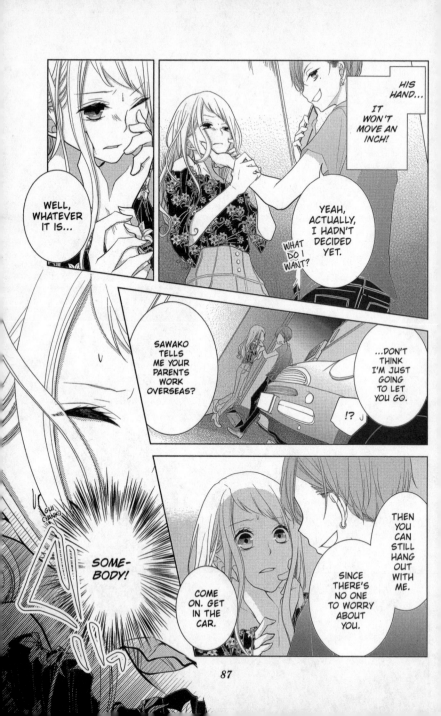

87

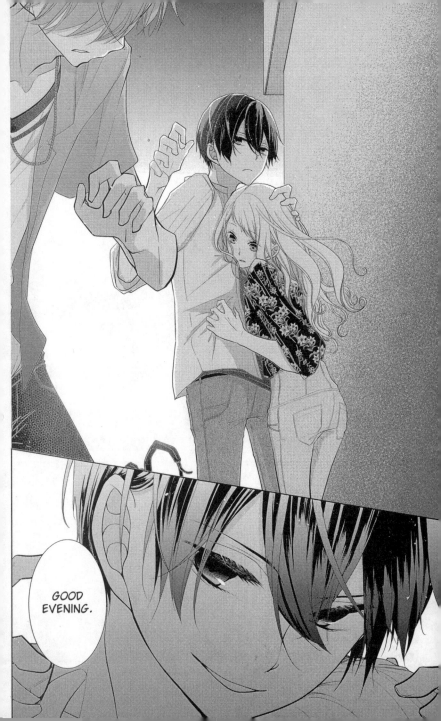

GOOD
EVENING.

HA...
...RUMA-KUN...

OH!

I WAS JUST GETTING SOME STUFF OFF HER FACE.

DID IT LOOK LIKE I WAS THREATENING HER!?

BA GRIN

TCH.

I'M SORRY.

SO—

IT LOOKED FOR ALL THE WORLD LIKE SOME GUY WAS THREATENING MY CHILDHOOD FRIEND...

...AND MY HANDS JUST MOVED ON THEIR OWN.

OH REALLY?

#23

H-HOLD ON...!

...YEAH.

BYE, YOH.

WELL, IT'S GETTING LATE, SO I'LL JUST BE TAKING HER HOME.

KURU
(WHIRL)

HUH? HE'S SO SPARKLY...

SEE YOU TOMORROW.

ZOKU
(SHUDDER)

...OF TELLING ME NOT TO TRY TO RUN?

...WHAT DO I DO...?

I DON'T WANT TO HAVE TO SEE THAT GUY TOMORROW...

IS THAT A ROUND-ABOUT WAY...

...NO, FIRST I'LL HAVE TO DO SOMETHING ABOUT SAWAKO...

IF HE HAS HER NUMBER, THERE'S NO TELLING WHAT HE COULD DO TO HER...

...YOH-CHAN?

OH...

S... SORRY. YOU JUST STARTLED ME A LITTLE.

YOU'VE BEEN AWFULLY QUIET. WHAT'S WR—

SO (TAP)

BIKU (FLINCH)

!?

SORRY.

I JUST THOUGHT THIS MIGHT HELP YOU CALM DOWN.

AWA (FLUSTER)

AWA

FUWA (FWAH)

HUH?

...UH...

TOKUN (BADUM)

TH... THA—

I SMELL COLOGNE.

...OF COURSE YOU ARE.

...HE REALLY DIDN'T DO ANYTHING TO YOU?

HUH?

IT'S WHAT HE WAS WEARING.

AFTER ALL, YOU DID PROMISE ME THAT YOU'D TALK TO ME IF ANYTHING HAPPENED FROM NOW ON.

UM, WELL...

KUNIE-SENPAI WAS KIND OF ALL OVER ME ALL DAY TODAY.

...BUT NOT IN A WAY THAT REALLY NEEDS MENTIONING...

Y... YEAH. I'M FINE...

I ASSUME I CAN HOLD YOU TO THAT?

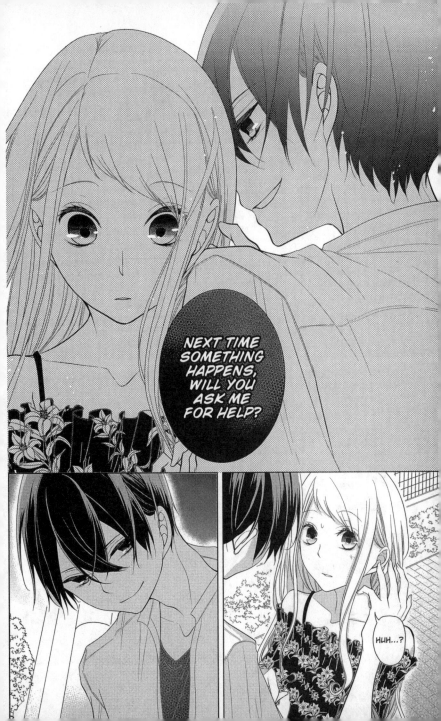

OH YEAH, DID YOU GO OUT TO EAT WITH TOUYA TONIGHT?

YEAH.

I'M JUST MESSING WITH YOU.

OH. IT WAS A JOKE...

HE MADE MY EARS TINGLE...

YOU HAVEN'T HAD DINNER, HAVE YOU, YOH-CHAN?

WELL, IT'S LATE. WE BETTER GET HOME.

I FOUND HIM AFTER SCHOOL, AND WE JUST WENT TO THE OKONOMIYAKI PLACE IN FRONT OF THE STATION.

I WAS ABOUT TO GO BACK TO THE SCHOOL, BECAUSE I FIGURED YOU'D STILL BE THERE, BUT...

WHAT!? YOU WERE GOING BACK!?

DID HE COME TO GET ME BECAUSE IT WAS SO LATE?

HE WAS CLOSER TO HOME. COULDN'T HE HAVE JUST GONE STRAIGHT BACK?

IT WAS INCREDIBLE. THERE WAS THIS BIG GRILL, AND THEY...

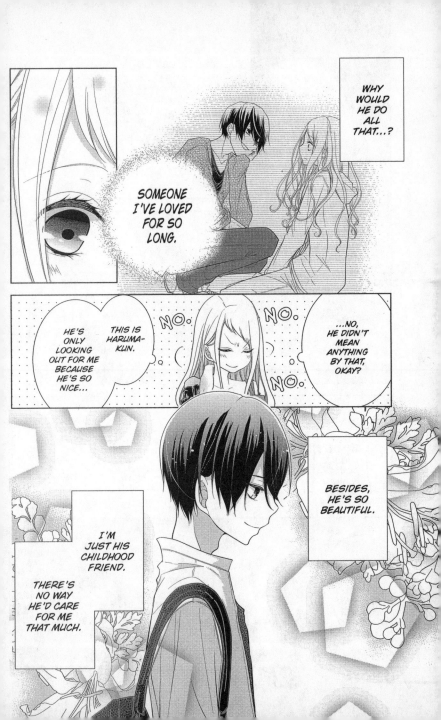

...PULL YOURSELF TOGETHER, YOH.

GU TCGNND

THIS IS JUST A MINOR PROBLEM.

FAVORITE SHOPS, THINGS LIKE THAT.

GOOD RESTAURANTS IN THE AREA.

HUH... THEY'RE ALREADY FRIENDS...

WHAT DID YOU AND TOUYA TALK ABOUT?

OH YEAH, HARUMA-KUN.

I HAVE TO HANDLE IT MYSELF.

WE PARTED WAYS AS SOON AS WE LEFT THE RESTAURANT.

JUST NORMAL STUFF.

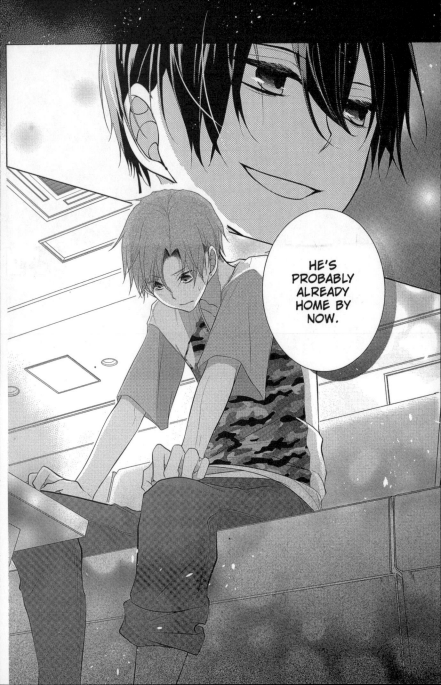

HE'S PROBABLY ALREADY HOME BY NOW.

#24

THREE HOURS EARLIER

JUUUUU (SIZZZZZZLE)

I MEAN, AT FIRST, IT WAS JUST...

WHY?

HOW IS THIS HAPPENING?

WHY ARE WE RANDOMLY...

OH, GO AHEAD AND PUT WHATEVER TOPPING YOU WANT ON FIRST.

IT'S MY TREAT TODAY.

...EATING OKONOMIYAKI?

...UMM.

...DIDN'T YOU CALL ME OUT HERE BECAUSE YOU HAD SOMETHING TO TALK TO ME ABOUT!?

KA! (BLUR?)

HUH?

WHOA, FOR REAL? OKAY...

YESSS!

WAIT, NO! I MEAN...

WHAAAAA?

I FEEL LIKE AN IDIOT FOR LETTING THAT TEXT FREAK ME OUT SO MUCH!!

I JUST WANTED TO HAVE A NORMAL CONVERSATION.

LIKE, I DUNNO... SOMETHING YOU CAN'T SAY TO YOH...

NO?

KERO (BLUNT)

DID MY INVITATION COME ACROSS WEIRD?

OH, I SEE.

THE TRUTH IS...

OR DID YOU HAVE SOMETHING YOU WANTED TO ASK ME ABOUT?

GAYA (CLAMOR)

GAYA

GAYA

HUH !?

NO... NOTHING. GAYA

NOT IN PARTICULAR.

I WANT TO ASK YOU EVERYTHING.

...OR HOW COME YOU REMEMBER HER WHEN SHE DOESN'T REMEMBER YOU.

...I WANT TO ASK HOW CLOSE YOU AND YOH WERE BACK IN THE DAY...

...AND SUDDENLY SHE TRUSTS YOU.

I SEE YOU SHOWING UP OUT OF NOWHERE, ACTING FRIENDLY...

BUT I...

I KNOW I'M BEING UNREA-SONABLE.

IT JUST BUGS ME FOR SOME REASON. THAT'S ALL...

BUT YOU REALLY AMAZE ME, TOUYA-SAN.

HUH?

IT'S NOT LIKE HE DID ANY-THING WRONG.

HEH.

I'M IM-PRESSED.

I CAN SEE WHY YOH-CHAN IS SO PROUD TO HAVE YOU AS A FRIEND.

SEE #6

I MEAN, YOU DID A STAKEOUT IN THE MIDDLE OF THE NIGHT TO HELP YOH-CHAN, RIGHT?

W... WELL, SHE IS MY BEST FRIEND.

YEAH, BECAUSE I SUSPECTED YOU.

ONE HOUR LATER

HEY. TELL ME WHERE YOU LIKE TO SHOP AROUND HERE.

HUH? OKAY.

WELL...

DOOON (DUDUN)

AFTER ALL MY WORRIES, HE REALLY JUST TREATED ME TO DINNER.

WELL, I'LL SEE YOU TOMORROW.

THANKS FOR COMING!

PATAN (SHUT)

SIGN: OKONOMIYAKI

OKAY, BE CAREFUL. THERE'S A LOT OF BARS AROUND HERE, SO IT'S EASY TO RUN INTO TROUBLE.

YEAH. YOU TOO, TOUYA-SAN.

...USED TO THE AREA...

NO, I'M...

ZAWA (MURMUR)

WHAT? YOU'RE NOT GOING THIS WAY?

THAT'S WHERE THE STATION IS.

I HAVE SOME-WHERE I NEED TO GO.

ZAWA

ZAWA

102

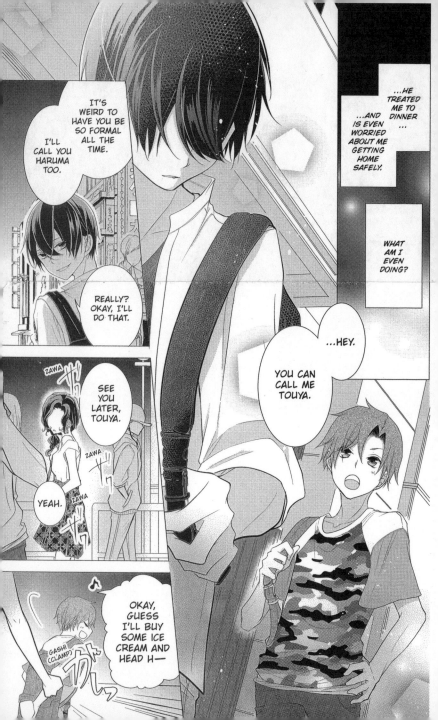

HM? YEAH. WHO'S ASK...

GASSHIRI (GLOMP)

TOUYA...

...ARE YOU TOUYA OOSHIMA-KUN...?

HUH?

HUH?

AND SO...

...ING?

SIGNS: KARAOKE PLAZA / KARAOKE / BEEF BOWLS

DOOON (DUDUN)

I'M SO SORRY FOR KEEPING YOU OUT WHEN YOU'RE TRYING TO GET HOME.

...HERE WE ARE.

I CAN'T BELIEVE I'M THE ONE WHO RAN INTO TROUBLE...

AT A KARAOKE BOX

YEAH, WHO ARE YOU ANYWAY?

OH!

I'M MADOKA SHIMIZU. A SOPHOMORE AT THE SAME COLLEGE AS YOU.

BUT I'M ACTUALLY TWO YEARS OLDER THAN YOU.

WE'RE IN THE SAME MAJOR, BUT I KNOW I CAN'T EXPECT YOU TO RECOGNIZE ME.

...HOW DOES AN UPPER-CLASSMAN KNOW MY NAME...?

HUH?

THERE ARE RUMORS ABOUT SOME HEROIC FRESH-MEN CAPTURING STALKERS AND PROWLERS AND STUFF.

THEY'VE BEEN GOING AROUND SINCE SPRING. HAVEN'T YOU HEARD THEM?

WHAT!?
I FEEL LIKE YOUR FACTS ARE KINDA JUMBLED.

WOW.

SOPHOMORE SOPHOMORE

THIS YEAR'S FRESHMEN ARE INTENSE.

OH, BUT I GUESS I DID TELL A FEW PEOPLE MYSELF.

OH! MY SITUATION ISN'T THAT SERIOUS.

JUST AN EX-BOYFRIEND WHO WON'T STOP FOLLOWING ME AROUND.

JUST TEXTING ME ALL THE TIME AND LYING IN WAIT FOR ME.

NO ILLICIT PHOTOG-RAPHY OR ANYTHING LIKE THAT.

!?

...I WAS THINKING THAT MAYBE YOU COULD GET RID OF MY STALKER TOO...

AND SO...

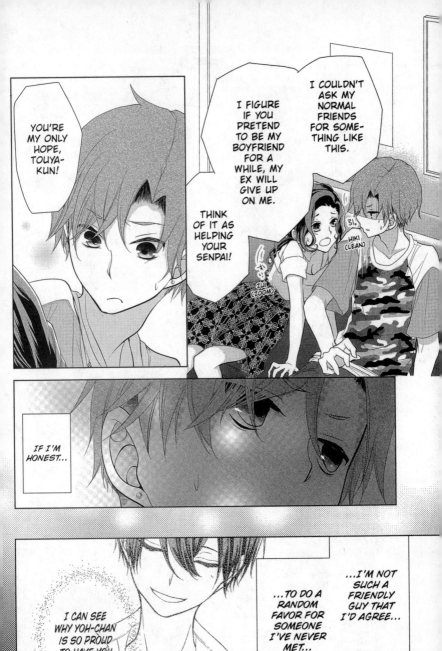

...I DON'T WANT TO LET HIM BE BETTER THAN ME IN ANY WAY.

...OKAY, FINE.

...BUT...

PAA (BEEEAM)

REALLY?

JUST FOR A LITTLE WHILE.

BUT WHEN THINGS CALM DOWN, YOU NEED TO MAKE SURE TO HAVE A REAL TALK.

DOOON (DUDUN)

BE-SIDES...

AND YOU CAN CALL ME MADOKA! ♡

NO THANKS.

THEN I'LL START CALLING YOU TOUYA!

THANK YOU!

GAH!

...I WANT...

...TO BE THE KIND OF PERSON WHO WILL BE A BEST FRIEND SUITABLE FOR A SOFT-HEARTED GIRL LIKE HER.

YOH WILL BE BUSY DOING STUDENTS' UNION STUFF FOR A WHILE ANYWAY.

WELL... I'M SURE IT'LL BE FINE.

WE CAN SPEND A LITTLE TIME APART.

THE NEXT DAY

GAYA
(CLAMOR)

GAYA

GAYA

...BUT THERE'S NO TELLING WHAT HE'LL DO IF I DON'T SHOW UP...

YOH!

THIS DAY WENT BY REALLY, REALLY FAST...

ZULULUN (GLOOOOOM)

I DON'T WANT...

...TO GO.

...ER. THE THING IS, SAWAKO...

LUCKY.

HYOKO (CHOP)

HUH...? UH...

HEY! YOU'RE GOING TO THE STUDENTS' UNION TODAY, RIGHT? RIGHT?

HE REALLY IS JUST AS NICE AS THE RUMORS SAY.

TWO GIRLS IN SAWAKO'S MAJOR

MAYBE IF I REALLY INSIST, HE'LL LET ME JOIN THE STUDENTS' UNION TOO! ♡

HEH HEH.

I BET YOU'RE JEALOUS.

I HEARD YOU GOT A RIDE HOME IN HIS CAR LAST NIGHT, SAWAKO?

YEAH, BUT IT WASN'T THE INFAMOUS LUXURY VEHICLE THAT COST EIGHT FIGURES.

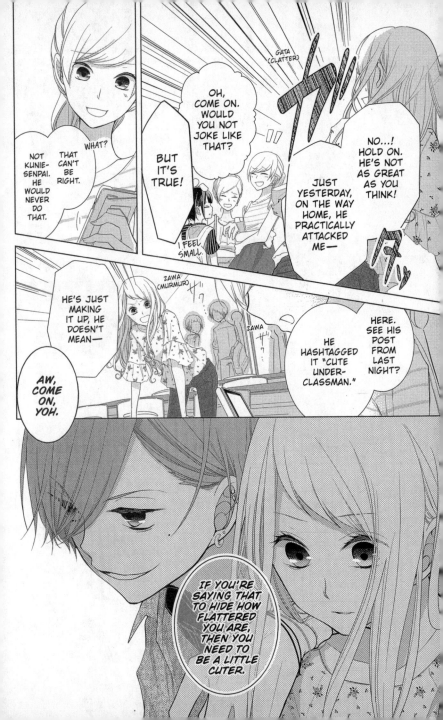

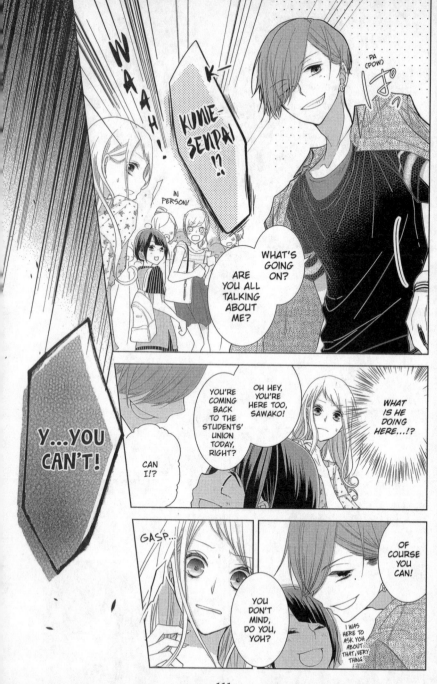

111

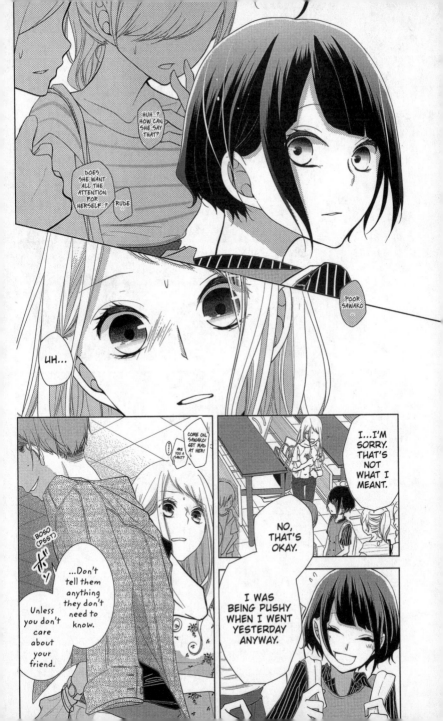

LET'S GO, SAWAKO.

?

...WHAT WAS THAT? THEY'RE GETTING ALONG FINE.

AND SHE KEEPS HIM TO HERSELF. SHE'S THE WORST.

GASP!

WELL, SEE YOU LATER, YOH!

...!

WE'LL GET SOME DONUTS

YAY!

...WHAT DO I DO?

GII (CREAK)

I WON'T GET TO CLEAR THINGS UP WITH SAWAKO...

...BUT MAYBE I SHOULD KEEP MY DISTANCE FROM HER UNTIL I GET THIS ALL WORKED OUT...

...BUT THERE'S NO TELLING WHAT KUNIE-SENPAI WOULD DO TO SAWAKO IF HE FINDS OUT I TOLD HER.

I COULD TRY TO EXPLAIN WHAT'S GOING ON...

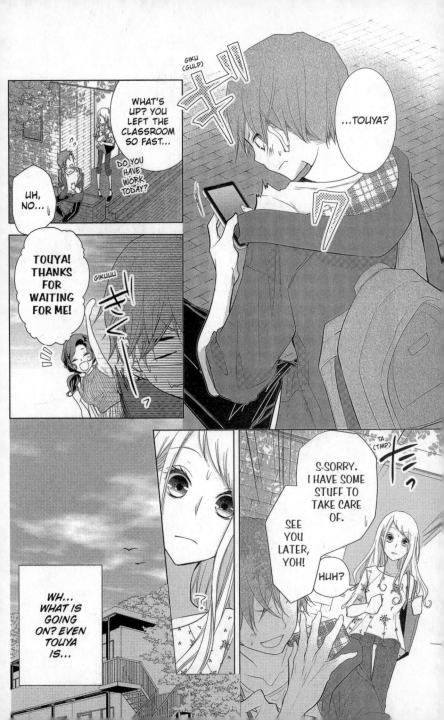

STUDENTS' UN

MAYBE IT WAS A GOOD THING I DIDN'T BRING TOUYA WITH US THE FIRST DAY.

...AND HAVING KUNIE-SENPAI FIND OUT WE'RE FRIENDS.

WELL... IT'S BETTER THAN HIM BEING SEEN WITH ME...

KAN (CLANG)

KAN

KAN

...OR HE'LL DRAG EVERYONE AROUND ME INTO THIS MESS.

I NEED TO GET AWAY FROM KUNIE-SENPAI, AND FAST...

KINOSHITA-SENPAI.

WHAT'S UP—

UM...

DOSA (THUD)

I NEED SOME KIND OF PROOF...

Y-YAGISAWA-SAN.

EVEN IF I TELL PEOPLE THE TRUTH ABOUT HIM, THEY'RE NOT JUST GOING TO TAKE MY WORD FOR IT.

GACHA (KACHAK)

OH!

115

HELLO, YOH-CHAN.

HARUMA-KUN...?

H...

HARUMA! YOU CAME!

GACHA (KACHAK)

WHY ...?

AH!

116

WHAT IS HARUMA-KUN DOING HERE...!?

SORRY TO KEEP YOU WAITING.

I WENT TO THE FRESHMAN CLASSROOM AND GOT CAUGHT TALKING TO PEOPLE.

IT'S FINE.

IS HE A FRIEND OF YOURS, YAGISAWA-SAN...?

...NO.

...BE FRIENDS?

NO.

HE ALWAYS DID LIKE PEOPLE WHO'D LOOK GOOD ON SOCIAL MEDIA.

SO HE SUPPOSEDLY PICKED ONE AT RANDOM, ASKED TO BE FRIENDS, AND BROUGHT HIM HERE.

...KUNIE WAS ALL, "WE NEVER GET MANY EXCHANGE STUDENTS AT OUR EVENTS."

OUT OF NO-WHERE...

HE SOUGHT HIM OUT.

JUST LIKE SAWAKO.

BECAUSE HE FOUND OUT YESTERDAY THAT HE'S MY CHILDHOOD FRIEND.

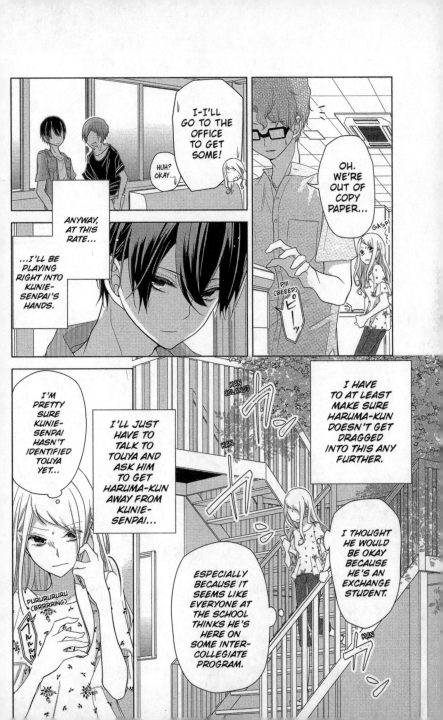

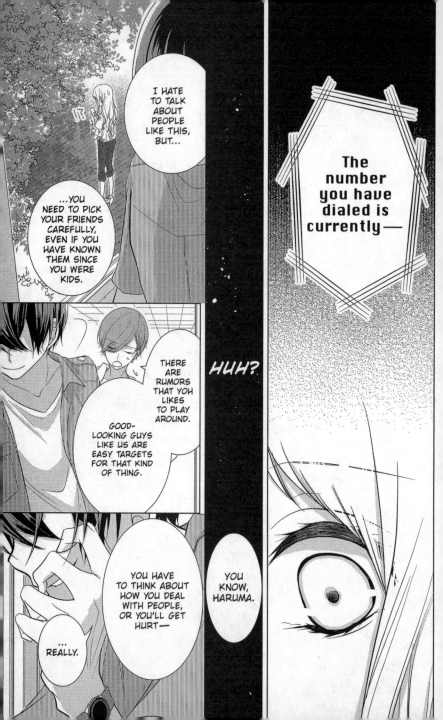

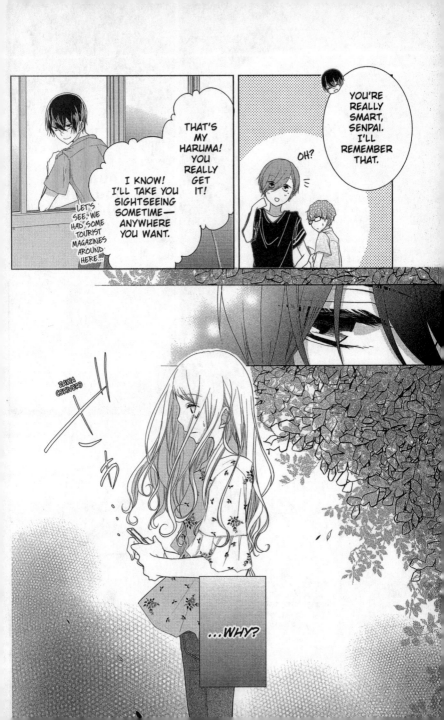

...COME TO THINK OF IT, WHEN KUNIE-SENPAI CAME TO OUR CLASSROOM A LITTLE WHILE AGO...

...I ASSUMED HE WAS THERE TO REMIND ME NOT TO RUN AWAY.

BUT WHAT IF HE WAS THERE TO DELIBERATELY RUIN MY REPUTATION IN FRONT OF SAWAKO...?

IF KUNIE-SENPAI SAID SOMETHING TO TOUYA, THAT WOULD EXPLAIN HIS WEIRD ATTITUDE...

AND NOW HE'S EVEN TAKEN HARUMA-KUN HOSTAGE.

ZAA (ZSHHH)

....

...I TRUST YOU, YOH-CHAN.

BOSO (PSST)

DOES THIS MEAN THAT RIGHT NOW...

...I HAVE ZERO FRIENDS?

MUU (POUT)

THAT'S WHAT YOU GET FOR CONSTANTLY FIDDLING WITH YOUR PHONE IN FRONT OF YOUR GIRLFRIEND.

HEY! MADOKA-SENPAI!

GIVE ME BACK MY PHONE.

NOPE.

#26

So I'm not supposed to contact her at all!?

AND HOW DO YOU KNOW, AFTER YOU TELL HER, THAT SHE WON'T GO BLABBING TO EVERYONE ELSE?

Yeah, because you told me not to tell other people that I'm pretending to be your boyfriend.

That's why I was texting her instead!

THAT'S JUST...!!

UHHH...

JUST TELL HER THAT YOU HAVE A GIRLFRIEND.

I'D BE OKAY WITH THAT.

GUSU (SNIFFLE)

URK!

...THIS ALL BACKFIRES, AND I GET STABBED, ALL BECAUSE OF YOU?

SO YOU WOULDN'T CARE IF MY EX LEARNS EVERYTHING...

HAPPENS ALL THE TIME IN SOAP OPERAS

I'LL KILL YOU AND THEN MYSELF!

AAAAH!

THAT HURTS! AM I NOT GOOD ENOUGH TO BRAG ABOUT!?

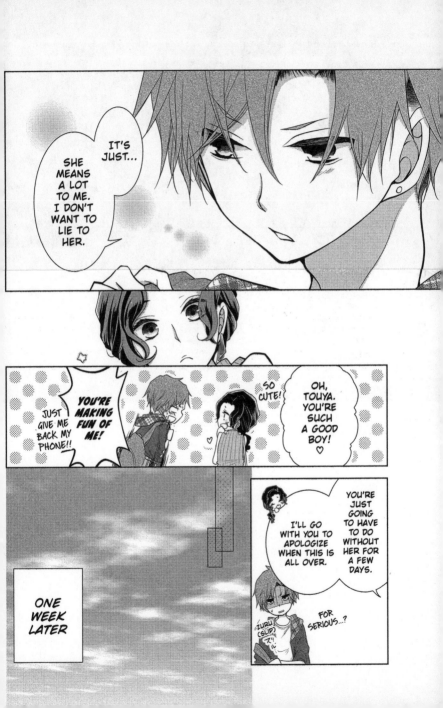

...AND ASK ME THAT?

YOU SEE ME HERE LIKE THIS...

THE HARASSMENT FROM KUNIE-SENPAI JUST KEEPS GETTING WORSE.

HEY, YOH.

AREN'T YOU DONE WITH THE CUE CARDS FOR THE STUDENT ASSEMBLY I ASKED YOU FOR YESTERDAY?

PATAN (SHUT)

OH, HARUMA? IT'S ME.

LET'S GO GET SOMETHING TO EAT.

KURU (WHIRL)

HUH? WHAT'S THIS? AM I SENSING THAT YOU WANT TO SAY SOMETHING?

...NO.

I DIDN'T THINK SO.

SINCE THAT FIRST DAY...

WELL, I'M GOING OUT FOR A BIT, SO CLEAN UP, WOULD YA?

NIYA (SMIRK)
NIYA

125

FOR NOW, I DON'T THINK SENPAI IS GIVING HIM THE SAME TROUBLE HE'S GIVING ME...

...HAS TURNED INTO A COMPLETE CELEBRITY AROUND CAMPUS.

NO WAY!

I HEARD THE'S A FOREIGN EXCHANGE STUDENT.

#SUPERHOTKOUHA
#CHILLINTOGETHE

#SHOPPINGWITHMAGUN
#CHICKSPICKIN

ON TOP OF THAT, THANKS TO SENPAI'S SOCIAL MEDIA, HIS NEW BEST BUD HARUMA-KUN...

...KUNIE-SENPAI HAS WORKED ME LIKE A DOG, WITH NOTHING I CAN DO TO ESCAPE.

YOU'RE ALL ALONE, YAGISAWA-SAN?

OH?

A-1001
CLASSROOM B

WHAT'S WORSE...

IT MUST BE NICE TO BE THE GIRL ALL THE GUYS LOVE.

GIRLS IN ASIAN STUDIES MAJOR WITH SAWAKO

WHY DON'T YOU GO FIND SOME GUY TO TALK TO?

POOR SAWAKO.

...THE HATE FROM ALL THE OTHER GIRLS IS ONLY GETTING STRONGER.

...SHE'S FRIENDS WITH THE FAMOUS EXCHANGE STUDENT TOO.

NOT ONLY DOES KUNIE-SENPAI DOTE ON HER...

I TRIED TALKING IT OVER WITH KINOSHITA-SENPAI A LITTLE WHILE AGO, BUT...

THE WORK FOR THE STUDENTS' UNION KEEPS PILING UP, AND I'M SLEEP-DEPRIVED ALL THE TIME.

I CAN'T TALK TO SAWAKO BECAUSE SHE'S HIS HOSTAGE, AND I HAVEN'T BEEN ABLE TO GET IN TOUCH WITH TOUYA AT ALL.

GOSH! (RUB)

...WELL, AS LONG AS SAWAKO IS OKAY...

I'M TOO SLEEPY TO FIGHT THEM.

SORRY...

HUH? ISN'T THIS THE TREASURER'S JOB...?

← HIS FAULT

...I DON'T THINK MY TESTIMONY WILL CARRY MUCH WEIGHT.

...HE REFUSED TO HELP, SO THERE'S REALLY NOTHING I CAN DO.

...IS MAKE SURE NOT TO PUT KUNIE IN A BAD MOOD.

SORRY, BUT...ALL YOU CAN DO...

GACHA (KACHAK)

IF I COULD AT LEAST CUT BACK ON THE UNION WORK...

I BETTER FIGURE SOMETHING OUT SOON, OR I'M GOING TO COLLAPSE...

...AND YOU KNOW, I'VE NEVER ACTUALLY SEEN KUNIE-SENPAI SITTING DOWN AND WORKING—

HARUMA-KUN!?

WHOA— YOUR CLOTHES...!

HUH? I'M HOME!?

WELCOME BACK.

UTO (DOZE)

...OOF.

POSU (PLOP)

EEP!

OH, SORRY.

I HEARD SOMEONE OPEN THE DOOR WITHOUT SAYING ANYTHING, SO I JUMPED OUT OF THE BATH TO CHECK IT OUT.

RIGHT BEFORE SHE HIT THE WALL

HM?

FU
(FZH)

7...

...ARE
YOU OKAY,
YOH-CHAN?

BY THE
WAY, YOU
ALREADY
PASSED
YOUR
ROOM.

UH.

THAT
STARTLED
ME...I'M
DEFINITELY
AWAKE
NOW...

SABA
(SWIP)

IF THE
STUDENTS'
UNION WORK
IS TOO MUCH,
I COULD SAY
SOMETHING
TO SENPAI
FOR YOU.

I JUST
FEEL LIKE
YOU HAVEN'T
BEEN ABLE
TO SLOW
DOWN AT ALL
LATELY.

AND PUT
SOME
CLOTHES
ON...

WHY
DO YOU
ASK...?

I CAN'T
TURN MY
HEAD...

UM...

DOKI
(BADUM)

WE HAVEN'T EVEN BEEN ABLE TO CHAT AT SCHOOL LATELY...

ARE YOUR EYES BLOODSHOT?

PA (DASH)
GACHA (KACHAK)

...THAT IF I GO CRYING TO HIM...

...HE'LL BE SO DISGUSTED THAT HE'LL HATE ME.

I...I'M OKAY! THINGS WILL CALM DOWN SOON.

....

GU (GNN)

I CAN'T HELP THINKING...

...I WANT TO DO EVERYTHING I CAN FOR MYSELF.

...I SEE.

ANYWAY, I'M SORRY FOR LEAVING YOU TO TAKE CARE OF ALL THE CHORES.

I'M PRETTY SURE...

FOR NOW, I'LL JUST PUT UP WITH IT UNTIL KUNIE-SENPAI GETS IT OUT OF HIS SYSTEM.

HE SHOULD GET TIRED OF IT SOON ENOUGH...

...IT'S A HABIT I DEVELOPED A LONG TIME AGO.

DON (BUMP)

ACK!

BASA (RUSTLE)

BUT...

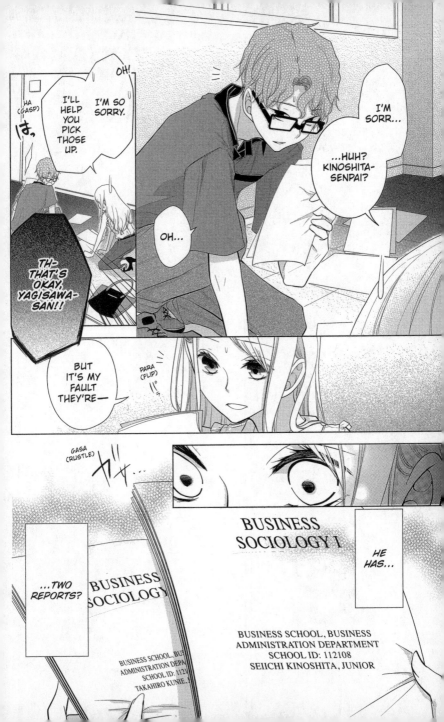

KINOSHITA-SENPAI, DON'T TELL ME...!

IS HE MAKING YOU WRITE HIS REPORTS!?

...IT'S FINE. I'M FINE.

FUI (STAND)

#27

......

YOU... HAVE KUNIE-SENPAI'S REPORT?

YOU DON'T HAVE TO TURN IT IN FOR HIM...

AH!

ALL THOSE PROPOSALS LYING AROUND THE STUDENTS' UNION ROOM.

THERE'S NO WAY KUNIE-SENPAI COULD HAVE WRITTEN THEM— HE'S ALWAYS GOOFING OFF.

THIS IS JUST TOO MUCH!

YOU HAVE TO TELL SOMEONE—

BA (BAM)

SO HE WAS MAKING OTHER PEOPLE WRITE THEM FOR HIM.

HOW CAN YOU LET HIM ...!?

IT'S NOT FINE.

I THOUGHT IT WAS STRANGE...

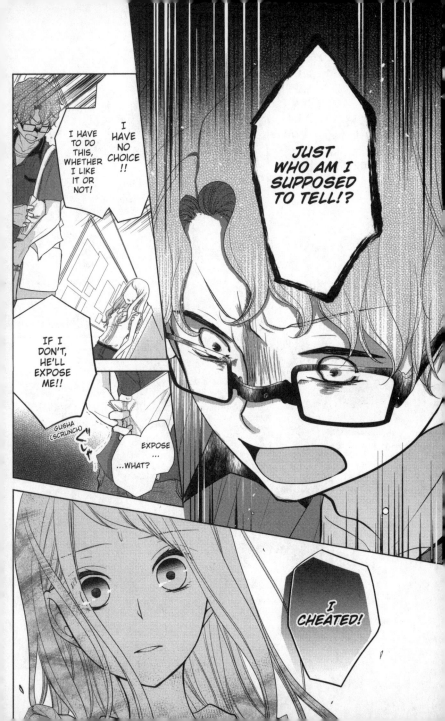

...IT WASN'T ALWAYS LIKE THIS. I DIDN'T START OUT AS HIS DOORMAT.

THERE WERE A LOT OF GOOD REASONS TO HANG OUT WITH HIM.

HE HAD MONEY, GOOD LOOKS, AND WAS FRIENDLY.

GIVE US A RIDE SOME-TIME!

YEAH, BUT OF COURSE I DON'T DRIVE IT TO SCHOOL.

WHOA! KUNIE, YOU HAVE A BMW i8?

BEFORE, I WAS JUST ONE OF THE MANY PEOPLE WHO FLOCKED TO BE NEAR HIM.

PERI (RIP)

...FINE. I'LL USE MY LAST RESORT.

BUT DURING FINALS OF OUR SOPHOMORE YEAR...

DAMN IT! JUST ONE QUESTION LEFT, BUT I DON'T KNOW...

IT'S JUST ONE QUES-TION...

HEY.

EST TIME
10:30
12:00

FIVE MINUTES TO GO...

WHATCHA DOIN', KINOSHITA?

...I SAW HIM FOR WHO HE REALLY IS.

THAT WAS WHEN...

IF YOU TURN ON HIM OR RUN FROM HIM, YOU'LL END UP LIKE TANAKA-KUN...

WHAT?

IF HE HAS DIRT ON ANYONE, THEY'LL BECOME HIS LACKEY WHILE HE PRETENDS THEY'RE HIS FAVORITE.

MOTODA AND TANAKA ARE IN THE SAME BOAT.

EVER SINCE, HE'S BEEN MAKING ME PUT MY NAME ON ALL HIS TESTS, AND HIS NAME ON MINE...

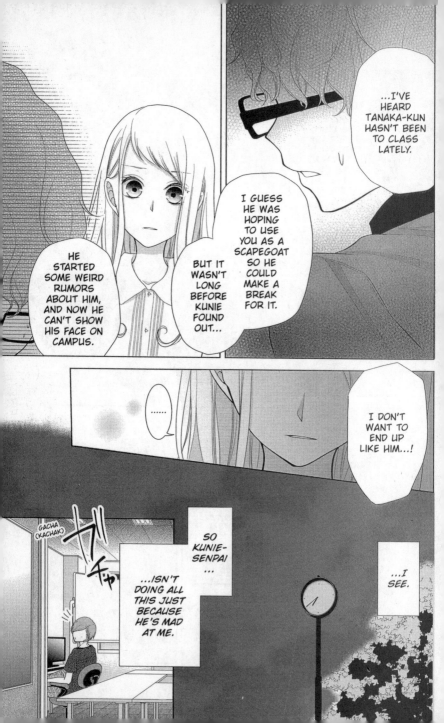

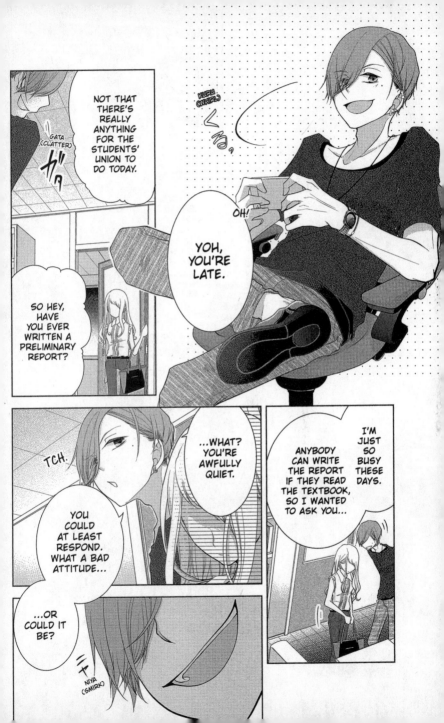

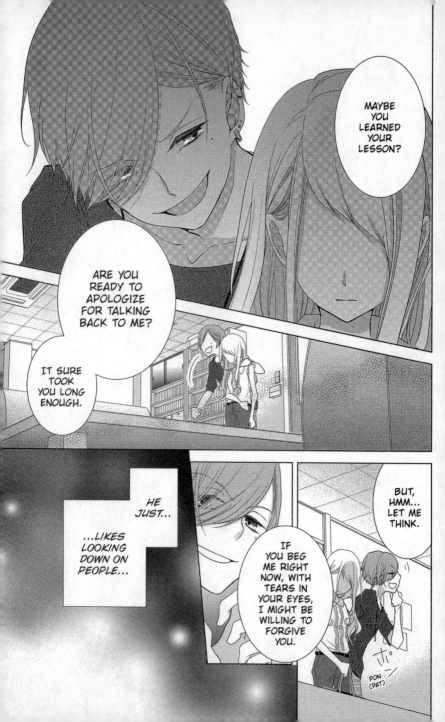

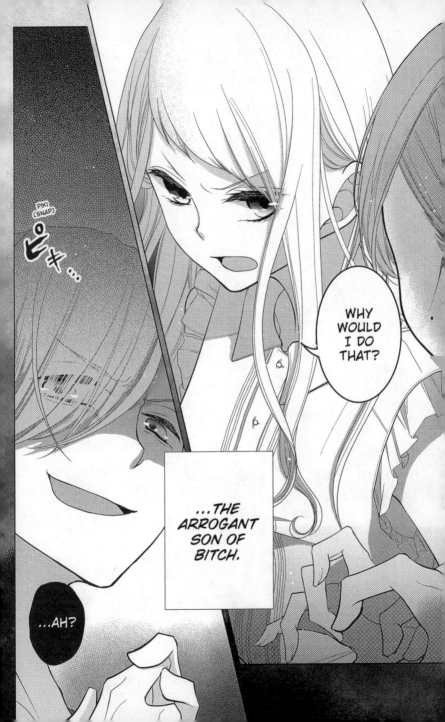

ESPECIALLY NOW THAT I'VE HEARD KINOSHITA-SENPAI'S STORY.

I THINK YOU'RE THE ONE WHO SHOULD FEEL SORRY, SENPAI.

YOU LITTLE... YOU GOT ALL QUIET, SO I THOUGHT YOU WERE ACTUALLY SORRY.

IRA (IRK)

BUT YOU JUST WANT TO TAKE THE EASY WAY OUT AND BLACKMAIL OTHER PEOPLE.

YOU LITTLE...

I WAS PUTTING UP WITH THIS BECAUSE I THOUGHT MAYBE I WAS KIND OF RUDE TO YOU.

AND I HAVE NO INTENTION OF BOWING TO YOU ANYMORE.

...WHA?

IF YOU'RE GONNA KEEP TALKING BACK TO ME LIKE THAT, I'LL MAKE SURE YOU'RE EVEN MORE ALONE.

GO AHEAD.

A FEW WORDS TO SAWAKO ABOUT YOU, AND TRUE OR NOT, SHE'LL—

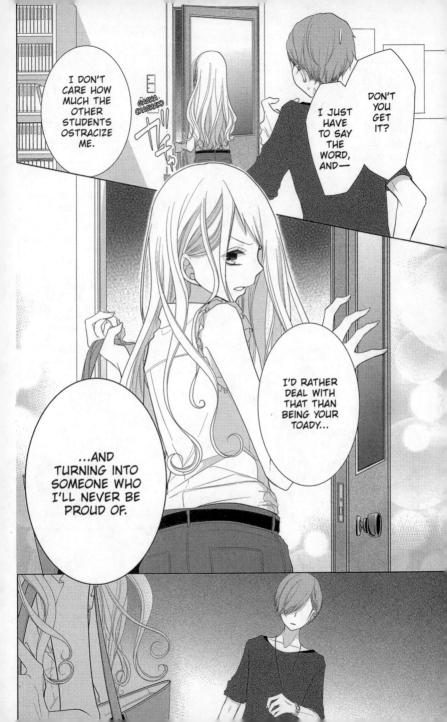

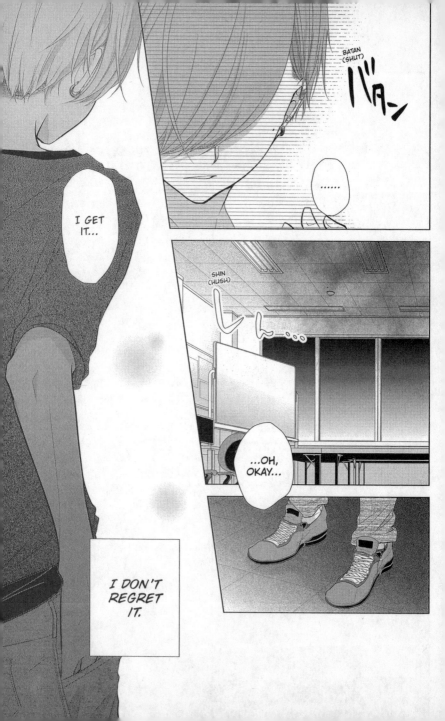

I'LL MAKE SURE YOU'RE EVEN MORE ALONE.

BECAUSE IT'S ALL TRUE.

...IF I KNOW KUNIE-SENPAI, HE MIGHT ACTUALLY TRY IT.

BUT I DOUBT HE COULD MAKE THE SITUATION ANY WORSE THAN IT ALREADY IS.

HISO (PSST)

ヒソ

HISO

ヒソ

HETARII (SLUMP)

へたーり…

...STILL.

IT WAS KINDA SCARY...

IF HE'D TRIED TO HIT ME, I'D HAVE BEEN IN REAL TROUBLE...

IT'S OKAY.

IT'S NOT LIKE THIS WILL GO ON MY WHOLE LIFE.

IT'S NOTHING ...

WILL YOU ASK ME FOR HELP?

...NO.

I'M OKAY.

AFTER ALL THESE YEARS, I DON'T WANT TO BE A WEAK LITTLE GIRL...

...WHO GOES CRYING FOR HELP OVER SOMETHING LIKE THIS.

IT'S NOT LIKE BEING ALONE IS NEW TO ME.

CRAP, IT'S ALREADY EIGHT O'CLOCK...

GAH!

BURORORO (VRROOOM)

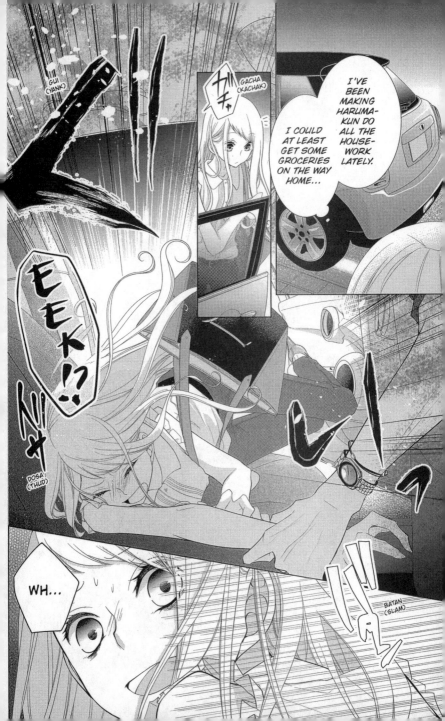

JIRO (GLARE)

WHAT...?

KUNIE-SENPAI!?

HA (GASP)

WAIT, YOH.

GIKU (GULP)

BA (WHOOSH)

I HAVE TO GET OUT...!

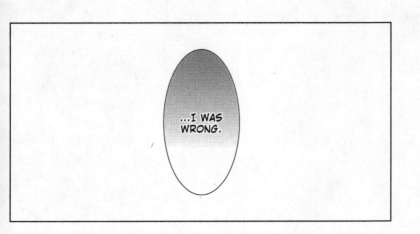

...I WAS
WRONG.

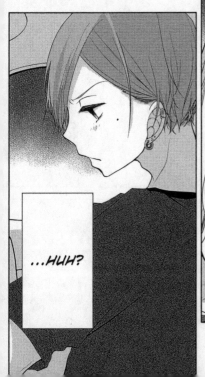

...HUH?

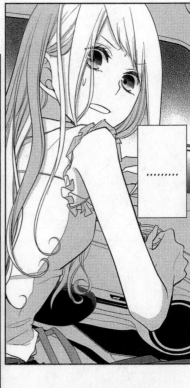

....

#29

WH... WHERE IS THIS COMING FROM...?
I SAID...
...I WAS WRONG. ABOUT ALL OF IT.
ALL... OF IT...?
...LIKE MAKING YOU GUYS MY MINIONS AND STUFF.
AND STUFF ...?
ALL THE BAD STUFF I DID!
I'M SORRY, OKAY!? I'M SORRY FOR ALL OF IT!
!?
!?
I'M NOT TOTALLY CLUELESS.
I KNOW I WAS BEING STUPID.
...BUT I CAN'T HELP IT.
WHAT? HE'S BEING SO HUMBLE ALL OF A SUDDEN...

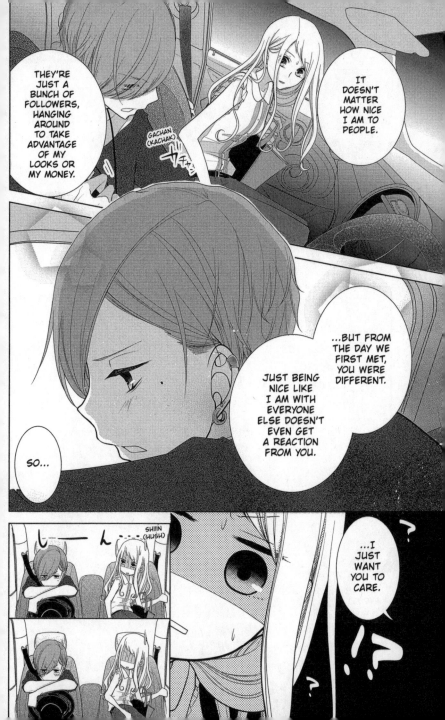

YOU LIVE ALONE, SO YOU KNOW WHAT IT'S LIKE, RIGHT?

SCARY...

GACHA

HUH?

I'M DRIVING YOU HOME!

PUT ON YOUR SEAT BELT ALREADY!

IT'S MY SORRY ATTEMPT AT TRYING TO MAKE IT UP TO YOU!!

I'D LIKE TO LEAVE.

...I DON'T UNDERSTAND HOW THAT WOULD MAKE YOU WANT TO BLACKMAIL PEOPLE.

CAN WE START HEADING BACK TO MY HOUSE NOW?

LIKE, YOU JUST WANT SOMEBODY TO BE THERE FOR YOU, SOMEONE WHO WILL ALWAYS BE ON YOUR SIDE.

I'LL KEEP THAT TO MYSELF!...

HARUMA-KUN HASN'T TOLD HIM THAT WE LIVE TOGETHER...?

MOST PEOPLE HAVE THEIR PARENTS, BUT THAT FEELING GETS WORSE WHEN YOU DON'T LIVE WITH THEM.

SIGN: ETC LANE

OH, SORRY. I WAS SO WRAPPED UP IN THE CONVERSATION, I ENDED UP ON THE HIGHWAY.

THE HIGH-WAY!?

THE TOLL ROAD

151

YOH! YOU WANT SOMETHING TO DRINK?

ENDED UP DRIVING FOR AN HOUR

ZAAN

ZAZAAAN (ZSHHH)

GAKON (KAKUNK)

WHERE IS THIS...?

I CAN SEE THE OCEAN...

IF THINGS GO BADLY, I COULD GET EXPELLED AND I'LL NEVER SEE YOU AGAIN.

I'M GOING TO TURN MYSELF IN TO THE PROFESSORS TOMORROW.

WHY? WE JUST GOT HERE.

CAN WE GO HOME NOW, KUNIE-SENPAI?

BATAN (SHUT)

HUH...?

GACHA (KACHAK)

COME ON. GIVE ME ONE LAST HURRAH.

I'VE NEVER REALLY BEEN THIS FAR OUT OF TOWN BEFORE...

ANXIOUS

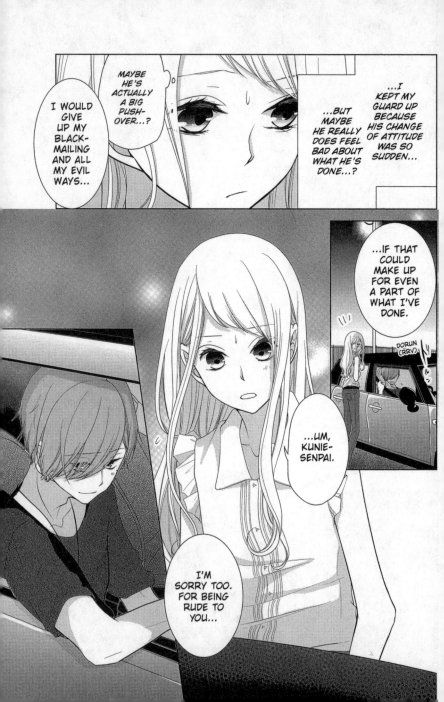

YOU SHOULD HAVE APOLOGIZED SOONER.
GAKON (KACLUNK)
YOU DUMB BITCH.

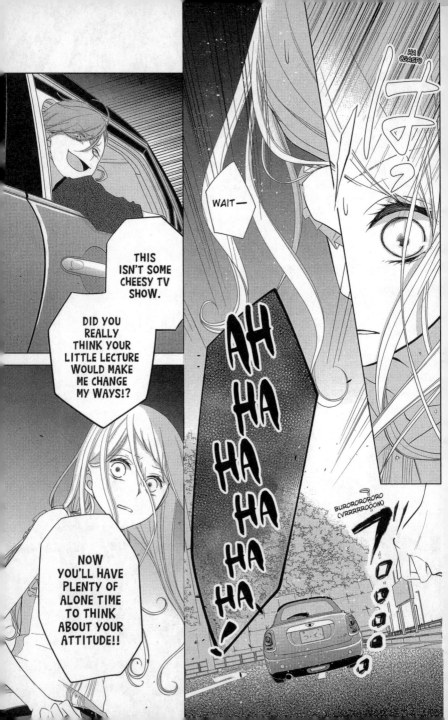

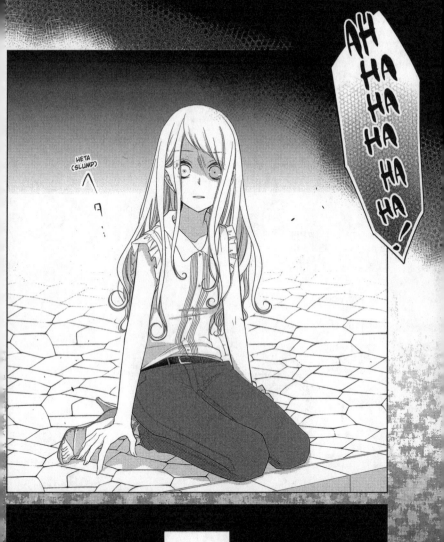

HA
(GASP)

SHIN
(HUSH)

#30

THIS PLACE IS DESERTED...

ZAZAN
(ZSHHH)

OF COURSE!

MY PHONE AND WALLET...

HOW AM I SUPPOSED TO GET HOME FROM HERE?

GAH! I LEFT MY BAG IN THE CAR...!!

20:56

LOW BATTERY

10% BATTERY REMAINING

DISMISS

AT LEAST I HAD MY SMARTPHONE IN MY POCKET.

BUT I'M ALMOST OUT OF JUICE...

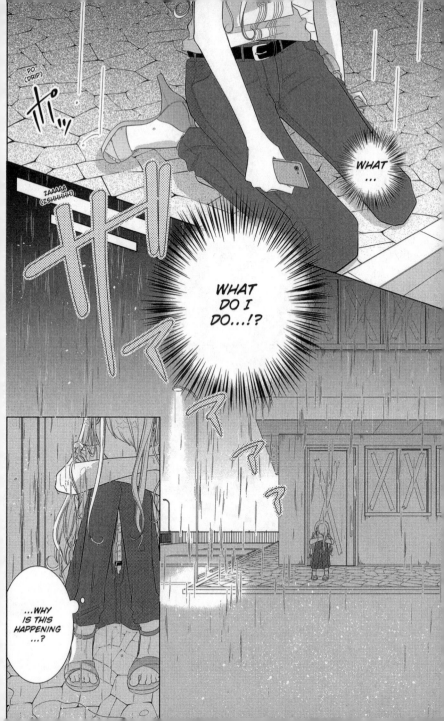

IS IT MY FAULT FOR LETTING THEM TALK ME INTO HELPING WITH THE STUDENTS' UNION?

OR FOR HELPING MY FRIENDS WHEN THEY WANTED ME TO TALK TO KUNIE-SENPAI IN THE LIBRARY?

...NO, STOP.

I MADE ALL THOSE DECISIONS MYSELF.

BUT...

A TAXI... WOULD COST MONEY, WHICH I DON'T HAVE, AND I DON'T KNOW THE AREA.

ANYWAY, I HAVE TO FIGURE OUT WHAT TO DO.

AND I JUST HATE THE IDEA OF CALLING SOMEONE AT THIS HOUR TO COME FIND ME IN THE MIDDLE OF NOWHERE...

TOUYA'S BEEN M.I.A. THE LAST FEW DAYS.

SAWAKO WAS WORRYING ABOUT ME THE OTHER DAY, BUT I TOLD HER I WAS FINE.

I'LL JUST HAVE TO CALL SOMEONE, TELL THEM WHERE I AM, AND HAVE THEM COME GET ME...BUT WHO?

SAWAKO
TODAY 21:11

I'M SORRY FOR YELLING AT YOU TODAY.

I'M SORRY TOO.
IF YOU'RE GOING TO BE BUSY, I'LL HANG OUT WITH GIRLS FROM MY MAJOR FOR A WHILE. YOU CAN COME HELP IF YOU NEED ME. IS EVERYTHING OKAY?

IT'S FINE, I'M FINE
I'LL CALL YOU WHEN
THINGS SETTLE DOWN

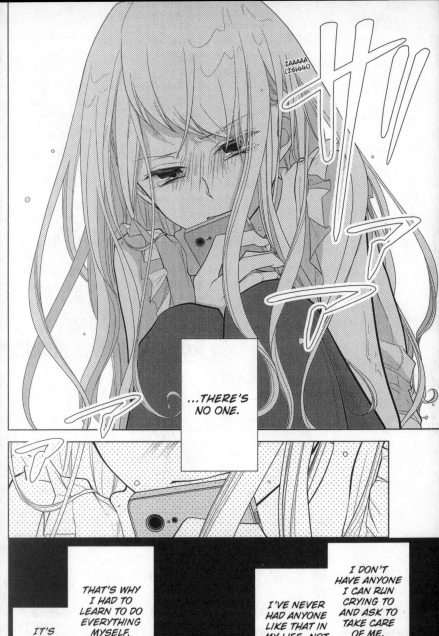

IF YOU'RE WORRIED ABOUT ANYTHING, I WANT YOU TO TALK TO ME ABOUT IT.

WHAT IF...

IF HE DID, THEN I...

PIRIRIRIRI
(RRRRING)

PURURURURU
(BRRRRING)

DO
(THMP)

DO

DO

WHAT IF...

HARUMA-KUN

MESSAGE   CALL   EMAIL

WHAT IF HE REALLY MEANT IT?

...HE WASN'T JUST SAYING THAT TO BE POLITE?

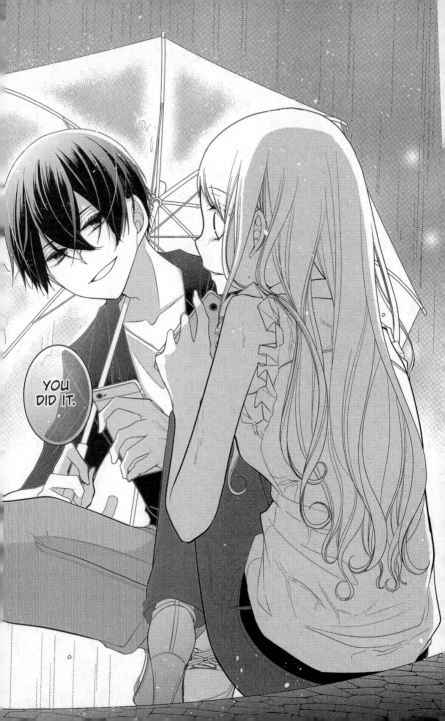

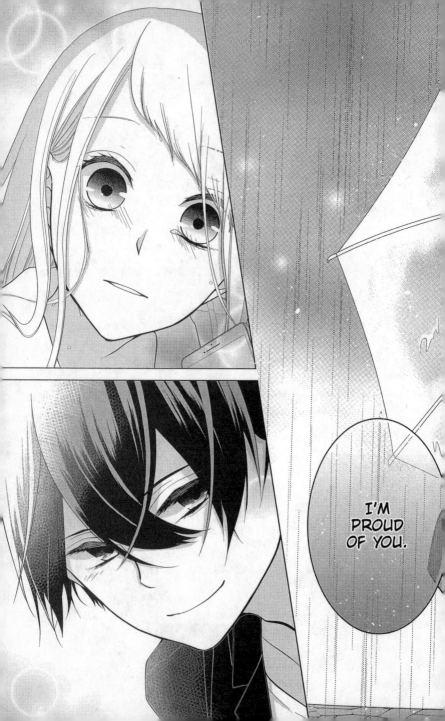

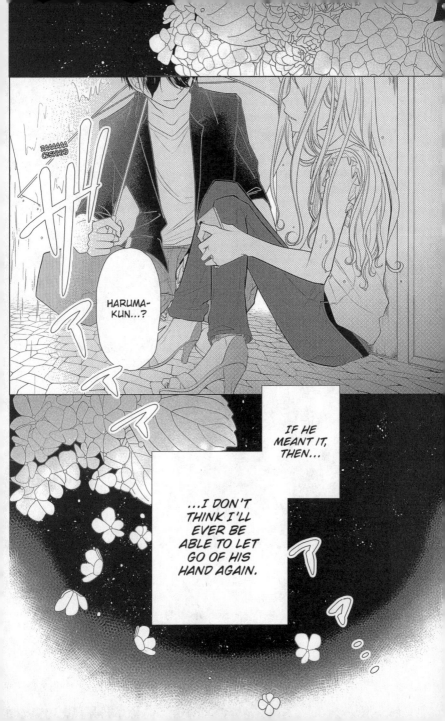

#31

...BUT... HOW?

HOW ARE YOU HERE, HARUMA-KUN...?

I HAPPENED TO BE NEARBY...

...WHEN KUNIE-SENPAI PULLED YOU INTO HIS CAR. I SAW THE WHOLE THING.

I THOUGHT HE MIGHT JUST BE DRIVING YOU HOME.

BUT SOMETHING SEEMED KIND OF WEIRD ABOUT IT...

...SO I JUMPED IN A TAXI AND FOLLOWED YOU.

I SURE WAS SURPRISED WHEN HE PULLED ONTO THE HIGHWAY.

ZAAAA

ザァァァ

165

IT SEEMS I MADE THE RIGHT CHOICE.

......

THE TAXI'S WAITING OVER THERE. LET'S GO HOME, YOH-CHAN.

I'M SORRY I DIDN'T REALIZE SOONER.

I CAN'T BELIEVE KUNIE-SENPAI WOULD DO SOMETHING LIKE THAT.

...ME?

166

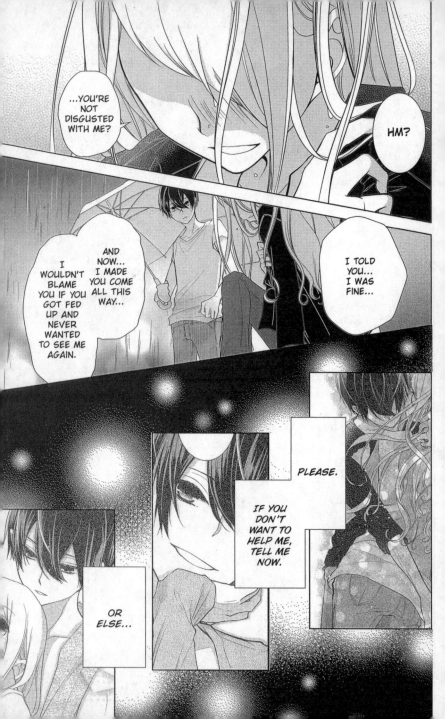

SU
(SFF)

...I'LL REMEMBER WHAT YOU SAID BEFORE, AND LET IT GO TO MY HEAD.

...WHY WOULD I DO THAT?

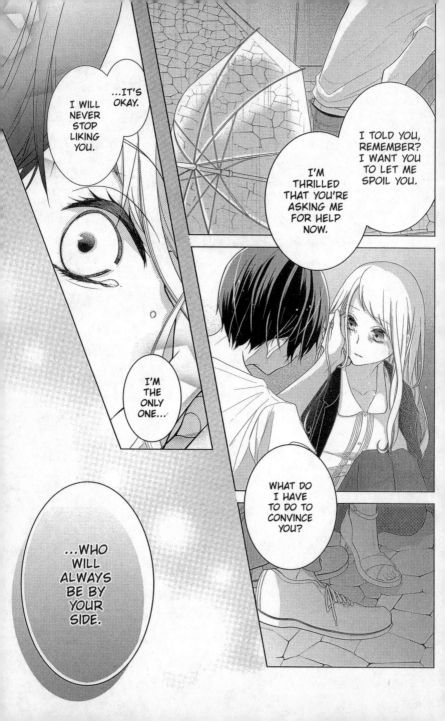

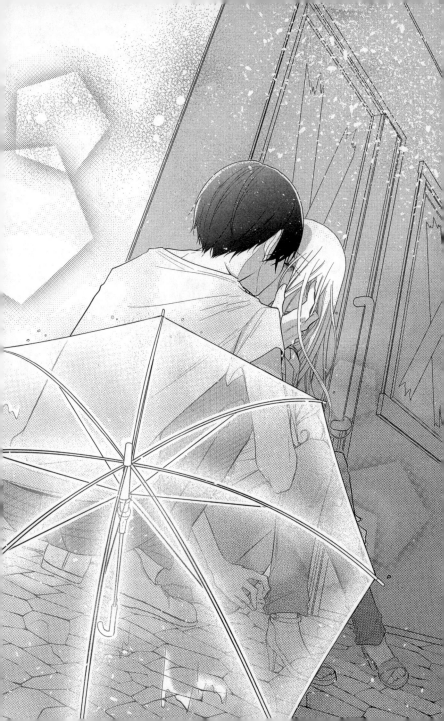

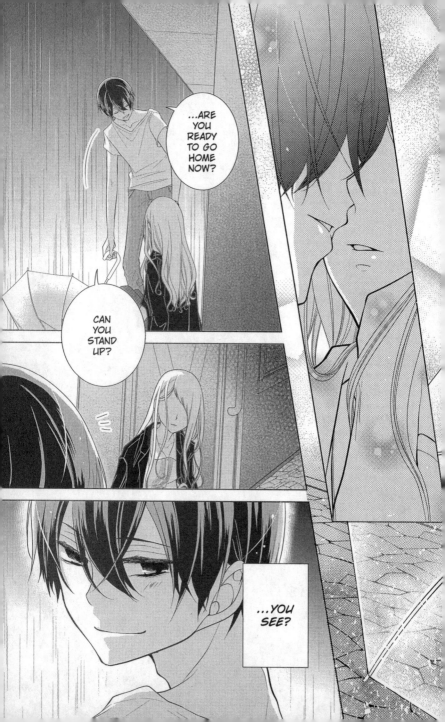

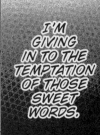

I'M GIVING IN TO THE TEMPTATION OF THOSE SWEET WORDS.

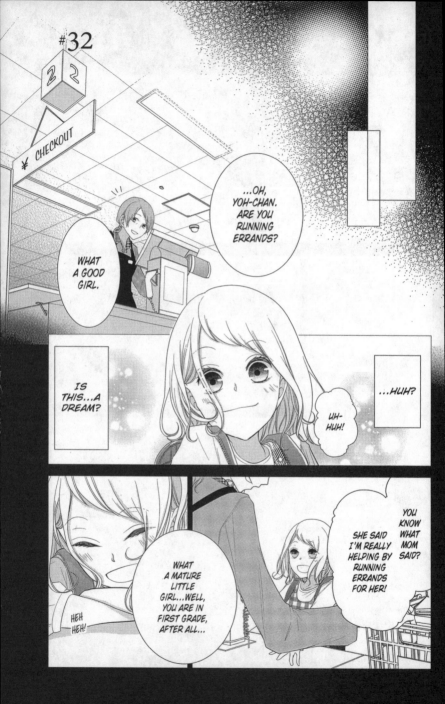

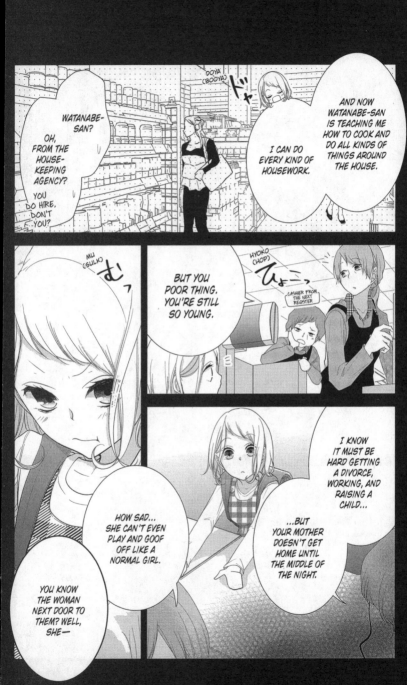

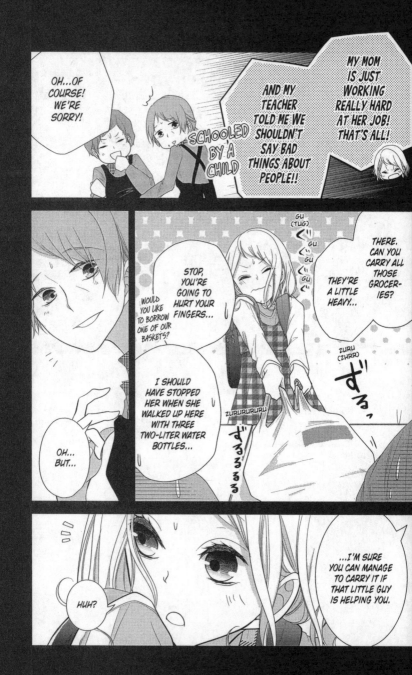

キャッシュコーナー　　夏ギフ

本
book

IF YOU BOTH CARRY IT TOGETHER—

...HUH?

I KNOW, RIGHT?

I WISH MY HUSBAND WOULD LEARN FROM HIM.

COME TO THINK OF IT...

...HOW DID I GET THOSE GROCERIES HOME?

AND BOTH OF US TOGETHER ...?

WHO WAS I "TOGETHER" WITH...?

...ALWAYS CRYING FOR HELP, ARE YOU?

SUKAAAA
(SNRRR)

I'M THE ONLY ONE WHO CAN HELP YOU.

BECAUSE I AM THE ONLY ONE WHO CAN UNDERSTAND YOU.

GURA
(SWAY)

I WANT IT THAT WAY.

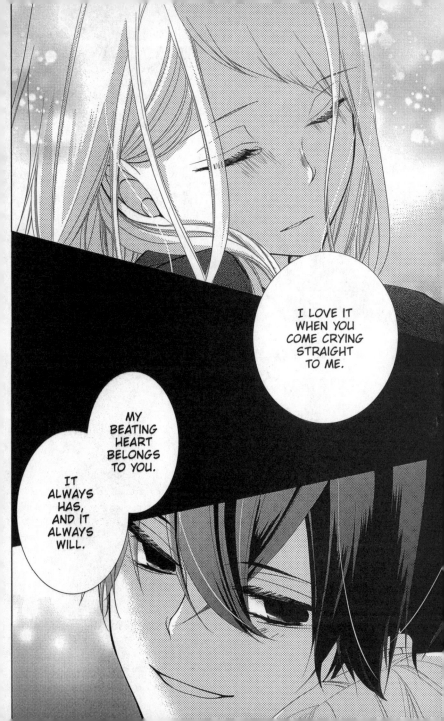

KUNIE-SENPAI

HARUMA!
WANNA HANG OUT
TOMORROW?
I ONLY HAVE CLASS
SECOND PERIOD!

21:44

KUNIE-SENPAI

PIRON
(DING)

MMM...

GURA
(SWAY)

KUI
(TUG)

...NOW,
THEN.

YOH-CHAN
CAME TO ME
FOR HELP,
LIKE SHE
PROMISED.

SO AS A
REWARD...

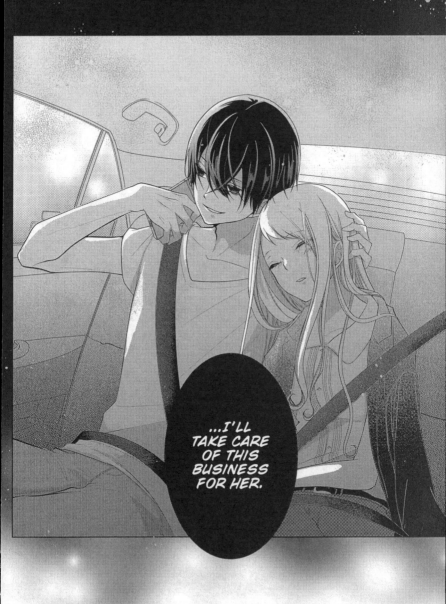

...I'LL TAKE CARE OF THIS BUSINESS FOR HER.

LOVE AND HEART ② END

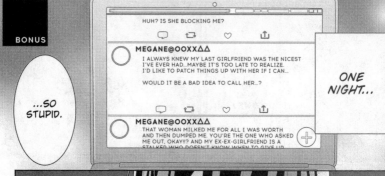

HUH? IS SHE BLOCKING ME?

MEGANE@OOXX△△
I ALWAYS KNEW MY LAST GIRLFRIEND WAS THE NICEST I'VE EVER HAD...MAYBE IT'S TOO LATE TO REALIZE. I'D LIKE TO PATCH THINGS UP WITH HER IF I CAN...

WOULD IT BE A BAD IDEA TO CALL HER...?

MEGANE@OOXX△△
THAT WOMAN MILKED ME FOR ALL I WAS WORTH AND THEN DUMPED ME. YOU'RE THE ONE WHO ASKED ME OUT, OKAY!? AND MY EX-EX-GIRLFRIEND IS A STALKER WHO DOESN'T KNOW WHEN TO GIVE UP.

...SO STUPID.

ONE NIGHT...

FIRST OF ALL, IT'S BEYOND TOO LATE.

AND SECOND, YOU'RE NEVER GOING TO GET SOMEBODY THAT GOOD AGAIN.

YOUR ACCOUNT IS NO

YOUR ACCOUNT WILL BE PERMANENTLY DELETED IN
IF YOU CHANGE YOUR MIND, YOU CAN REACTIVATE I
IN BEFORE YOUR ACCOUNT IS DELETED PERMANENT
CLICK HERE TO SIGN UP FOR A NEW ACCOUNT.

KATA
(TAPPP)

HIS ACCOUNT'S BEEN HACKED AND HE'S STILL USING IT? THIS EX-BOYFRIEND REALLY IS NOT VERY BRIGHT.

I WOULDN'T WANT YOH-CHAN TO READ THIS. IT MIGHT PUT HER IN A FORGIVING MOOD.

I'LL JUST DELETE THE WHOLE ACCOUNT.

...WHY WAS YOH-CHAN DATING A GUY LIKE HIM ANYWAY?

I'M GLAD I TOOK THE PRECAUTION TO BLOCK HIM.

181

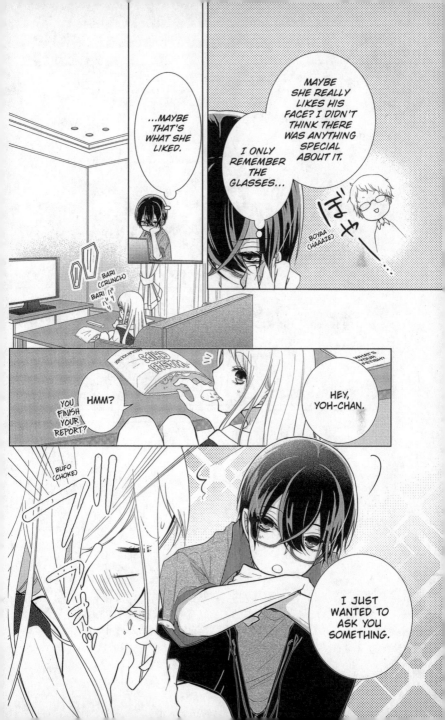

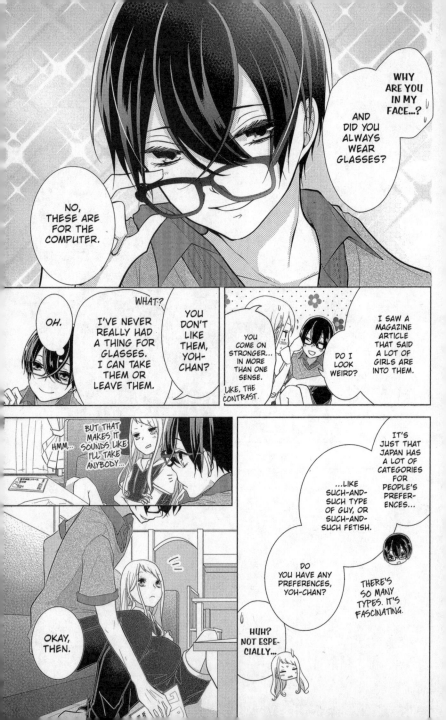

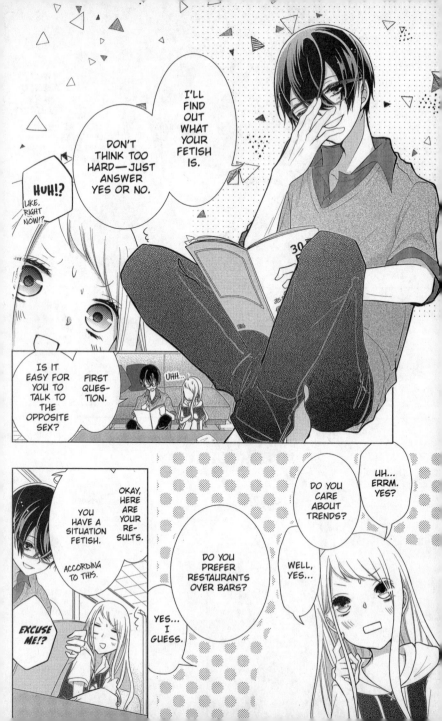

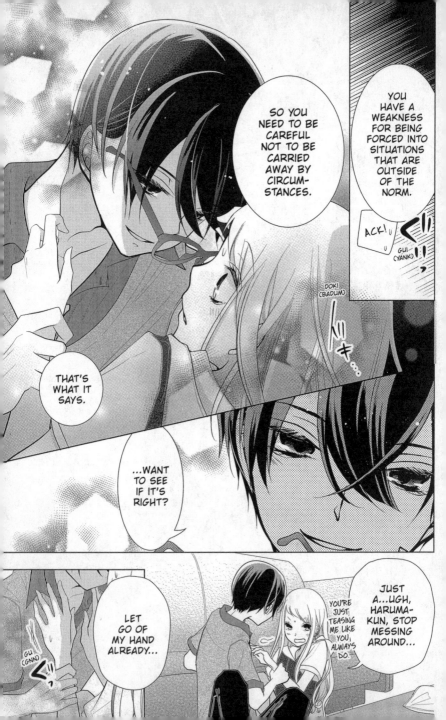

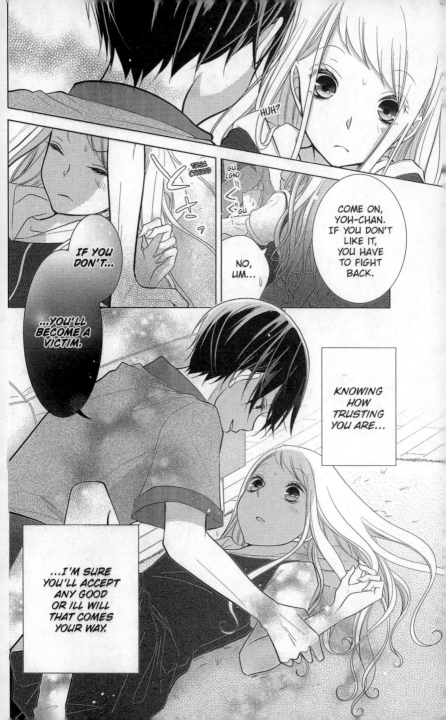

SO...

......

...OKAY, FINE.

HARUMA-KUN... LET ME SEE YOUR FACE.

MUGU (MRPH)

WHAT...?

TSUUN (STING)

I WAS KIND OF HOLDING BACK BECAUSE I KNEW I'D FEEL BAD FOR YOU.

BUT IT DOESN'T TAKE LONG TO FIGURE OUT WHAT SOMEONE DOESN'T LIKE WHEN YOU LIVE WITH THEM.

WASABI-FLAVORED POTATO CHIPS

NOT USED TO WASABI & CAN'T TAKE THE HEAT

WASABI!!

BUTSU (MUTTER)

HE ALWAYS TEASES ME LIKE THAT...

SHE'S TOUGH...

I'M SORRY...

BUTSU

HMPH!

ANY MORE SHENANIGANS, AND I SHOVE A WHOLE TUBE OF WASABI IN YOUR MOUTH.

BUT YOU HAVE THIS BIZARRE INNER STRENGTH. I CAN'T STAND IT.

...YOU'RE WEAK, TRUSTING, AND GULLIBLE.

...AND SODA.

HERE'S SOME WATER...

BECAUSE I BET...

...THAT'S WHAT DRAWS SO MANY PEOPLE TO YOU.

GRR...

IT WAS HIS ONLY WEAKNESS...!!

THIS SASHIMI IS GOOD.

WASABI SOY SAUCE

INCIDENTALLY, HARUMA EVENTUALLY CONQUERED WASABI.

BONUS / END

The Phantomhive family has a butler who's almost too good to be true...

...or maybe he's just too good to be human.

Black Butler

YANA TOBOSO

VOLUMES 1-29 IN STORES NOW!

LOVE and HEART

2

CHITOSE KAIDO

Translation: **ALETHEA AND ATHENA NIBLEY**

Lettering: **CHIHO CHRISTIE**

KOI TO SHINZO by Chitose Kaido
© Chitose Kaido 2019
All rights reserved.
First published in Japan in 2019 by HAKUSENSHA, INC., Tokyo.
English translation rights in U.S.A., Canada and U.K. arranged with HAKUSENSHA, INC., Tokyo through TUTTLE-MORI AGENCY, INC., Tokyo.

English translation © 2021 by Yen Press, LLC

Yen Press
150 West 30th Street, 19th Floor
New York, NY 10001

Visit us at yenpress.com
facebook.com/yenpress † twitter.com/yenpress
yenpress.tumblr.com † instagram.com/yenpress

First Yen Press Edition: June 2021

Yen Press is an imprint of Yen Press, LLC.
The Yen Press name and logo are trademarks of Yen Press, LLC.

The publisher is not responsible for websites (or their content) that are not owned by the publisher.

Library of Congress Control Number: 2020950226

ISBNs: 978-1-9753-2044-7 (paperback)
978-1-9753-2045-4 (ebook)

10 9 8 7 6 5 4 3 2 1

BVG

Printed in the United States of America

TRANSLATION NOTES

Common Honorifics
no honorific: Indicates familiarity or closeness; if used without permission or reason, addressing someone in this manner would constitute an insult.
-san: The Japanese equivalent of Mr./Mrs./Miss. If a situation calls for politeness, this is the fail-safe honorific.
-sama: Conveys great respect; may also indicate that the social status of the speaker is lower than that of the addressee.
-kun: Used most often when referring to boys, this indicates affection or familiarity. Occasionally used by older men among their peers, but it may also be used by anyone referring to a person of lower standing.
-chan: An affectionate honorific indicating familiarity used mostly in reference to girls; also used in reference to cute persons or animals of either gender.

Page 53
Senpai is a term commonly used to respectfully refer to upperclassmen in school or seniors at work. Its antonym, used for underclassmen, is *kouhai*.

Page 61
Izakaya are a type of Japanese bar that focus on serving small portions of side dishes designed to go with alcohol.

Page 67
Many official documents in Japan are dated using the *nengo* system for Japanese era names, based on the current ruling emperor. In this case, *Heisei 29* refers to the year 2017.

Page 95
Okonomiyaki is a type of savory cabbage and butter pancake made with a wide variety of ingredients. While popular in the Hiroshima and Kansai regions, it is available throughout Japan, with many local variations.

BUNGO
STRAY DOGS

P9-CQC-565

Volumes 1–19
available now

BUNGO
STRAY DOGS 01

Story by KAFKA ASAGIRI Art by SANGO HARUKAWA

If you've already seen the anime, it's time to read the manga!

Having been kicked out of the orphanage, Atsushi Nakajima rescues a strange man from a suicide attempt— Osamu Dazai. Turns out that Dazai is part of a detective agency staffed by individuals whose supernatural powers take on a literary bent!

www.yenpress.com

Yen Press